Midsomer Murders
on
Location

Sabine Schreiner
Joan Street

Edited by
Antony J. Richards

All correspondence for
Midsomer Murders on Location
should be addressed to:

Irregular Special Press
Endeavour House
170 Woodland Road
Sawston
Cambridgeshire
CB22 3DX

✳✳✳✳✳ ⭘ ✳✳✳✳✳

ISBN: 1-901091-37-6 (10 digit)
ISBN: 978-1-901091-37-3 (13 digit)

✳✳✳✳✳ ⭘ ✳✳✳✳✳

Cover Illustration: John Nettles and Daniel Casey in the roles of DCI
Tom Barnaby and DS Gavin Troy respectively taken while filming at
Hambleden.(see page 36).

✳✳✳✳✳ ⭘ ✳✳✳✳✳

✳✳✳✳✳ ⭘ ✳✳✳✳✳

CONTENTS

Contents

---

[1] Turville straddles the border of Buckinghamshire and Oxfordshire and is listed under the latter on the basis of Royal Mail, church and electoral register records.

4

INTRODUCTION

The fictional county of Midsomer and the people in it, originally created by Caroline Graham, first appeared on British television screens in 1997, thanks to Brian True-May and Betty Willingale. Having read the books, Betty Willingale realised their television potential, and convinced Brian True-May to borrow £1.5 million from the bank to produce the first episode, *The Killings at Badger's Drift*. They convinced John Nettles to leave the theatre for a short break, and take on the role of DCI Tom Barnaby – even Caroline Graham, the creator of this most unusual policeman, has said she can't imagine someone else in the role. Further inspired casting, helped by casting director Joyce Nettles, made the larger-than-life figures from the books come to life on the small screen.

It was an instant success, and today, some eighteen years on (and yes, John Nettles took that short break from the theatre for fourteen years and eighty-one episodes before handing over to Neil Dudgeon in 2011), the series is being sold into over two hundred countries worldwide – "to all countries that have televisions and even the ones where they wind them up", as Brian True-May only half-jokingly states. At the time of writing series seventeen is almost complete, which will bring the number of episodes made to one hundred and five. Long may they continue!

Every episode takes about five weeks to make, and costs around £1.3 million to produce. During a normal on set day, there may be about a hundred people, from actors to runners, make-up artists to directors, making the magic happen that is *Midsomer Murders*. Often, many hours on set will produce only a few minutes of footage in the final product. The series has attracted notable guest stars, from Honor Blackman of *Goldfinger* fame, to Orlando Bloom, before he appeared in *Pirates of the Caribbean* and the *Lord of the Rings* trilogy. Stars like Roger Moore and Johnny Depp have said they would like to spend some time in Midsomer county, and John Nettles has remarked that for him, this work was more like a very long party, with his favourite actors coming through the door every few weeks.

The mixture of a classic 'whodunnit', bizarre characters, storylines that often have a twist (or sting) in the tail and very talented actors has brought the series a loyal fan following around the globe. Everybody involved in making this well-loved television series though, from the actors to the producer, is unequivocal in naming the real star – the beautiful real-life setting of the fictional county to which this book is dedicated. Enjoy!

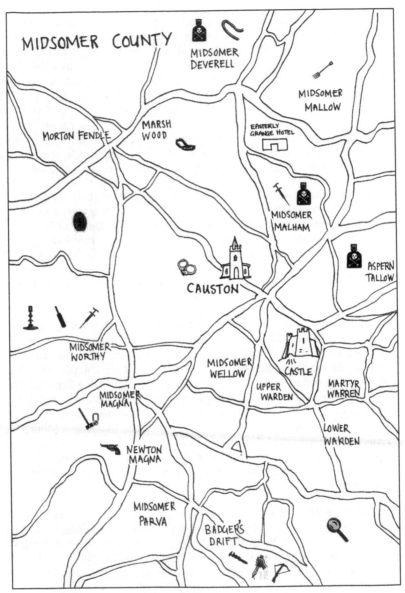

[Map of Midsomer County]

MIDSOMER COUNTY

The pretty villages that make up Midsomer county are strewn mainly over four counties; Berkshire, Buckinghamshire along the Chiltern range of hills, Hertfordshire and Oxfordshire but there have been some excursions to Surrey and even further afield as well, such as in *Death and Dust* to the Snowdon National Park in Wales, or Beer in Devon for *Down Among the Dead Men* and even Honfleur in France. But don't be fooled – often DCI Barnaby and his faithful sergeant will drive around a corner and make a very fast move from one village to another, if not even from one county to another. For some scenes, several locations have been used, for example in *Ring Out Your Dead* parts of no less than three churches were used to represent one building.

This guide shows some of those gorgeous filming locations, hopefully inspiring the reader to visit – be assured, they are all well worth one – and not just for the ardent fans of the series, but also in their own right.

Here, arranged alphabetically by county for convenience, are over one hundred of those magnificent locations used in filming *Midsomer Murders*. Rather than just list the places, the authors have tried to give the reader added information about their history, what to see and how to plan your own visit to Midsomer county!

MIDSOMER COUNTY OF BERKSHIRE

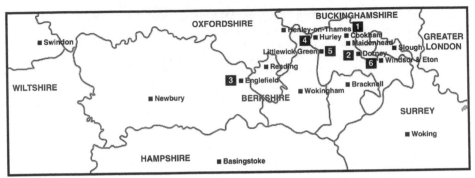

[Map of the Midsomer County of Berkshire]

Key to Symbols

	Building (large or important)		Building (general place or structure)		Church (religious establishment)		
	Hotel or Public House		Shop		Village Green		
	Village Hall						

Key to Map

1	Cookham (9)		4	Hurley (12)	
2	Dorney (10)		5	Littlewick Green (14)	
3	Englefield (12)		6	Windsor & Eton (15)	

COOKHAM - THE CROWN PUBLIC HOUSE HIGH STREET

Cookham has been a settlement site for some four thousand years, evidenced by three Bronze Age barrows and two megaliths in the vicinity. Its name derives from the Celtic *Cwch-ium* (which means 'Boat-Place'). The Romans and Saxons used an old River Thames crossing here, part of the Camlet Way that ran from Silchester to Verulanium in Hertfordshire (now known as St. Albans).

[The Crown public house]

The earliest mention of the village is in a charter dated 726. Alfred the Great fortified Cookham in 886 after the Vikings rowed up the River Thames in 870. The Saxon Kings had a Royal Palace in the area from sometime between 965 and 975, and the Witan (the Saxon parliament) met here in 997. In the Domesday book (1086), Cookham appears as Cocheham.

It lost both its strategic and economic value around 1250 when a wooden bridge was constructed in nearby Maidenhead, which made crossing the river much easier than using the Cookham ferry. The bridge at Cookham wasn't built until 1867 and a toll was charged to use it, right up to 1950. The old tollhouse still stands as a reminder of those times.

Several famous people are linked with the area. One of Britain's most renowned 20th century artists, Stanley Spencer, came from Cookham and some of his paintings were set in the village. A Wesleyan chapel, built in 1846, now houses the Stanley Spencer Gallery. He died in 1959 and there is a memorial stone in Cookham churchyard. Guglielmo Marconi (1874-1937), a pioneer of wireless communication, lived in Cookham Rise, where he is thought to have conducted experimental transmissions in 1897. Kenneth Grahame wrote *The Wind in the Willows* whilst living with his grandmother in nearby Cookham Dean and attending Herries School.

Of interest to film buffs, during World War II the J. Arthur Rank Organisation evacuated the whole of their London staff to Cookham's Moor Hall. Afterwards, a new company, Gaumont British Animations, produced the *Animaland* cartoons here.

Midsomer Murders came to Cookham in autumn 2002 to film scenes for the episode *Second Sight*. Barnaby comes to meet Cully and Joyce at The Crown public house that lies near the River Thames flood meadows. Also brief scenes of the High Street are seen when Scott phones Barnaby on his mobile telephone after visiting a solicitor there.

DORNEY - DORNEY COURT

[Dorney Court]

Dorney Court, a Grade I listed building, has been the home of the Palmer family for the last four hundred and fifty years. This fascinating Tudor building is situated in the village of Dorney, just a few miles away from Windsor Castle and Eton, squeezed between the River Thames and the M4 motorway.

Dorney is mentioned in the Domesday book as Dornei, which is Old English in origin, meaning 'island frequented by bumble bees' – the location of the village was once no more than a patch of hard ground in the middle of a swampy bog.

The outside of the house has changed through the centuries; the Tudor front was replaced in the 1730s with a Georgian façade, which in turn was replaced with another Tudor façade in the 1900s. Today, brick façades are carried on wooden beams and, coupled with the different size bays, once again give the house an authentic Tudor look. The inside is still mostly unchanged from the 1500s.

The house, set in beautiful grounds, contains some fine paintings, including portraits of many members of the Palmer family, and period pieces. There is a large stone pineapple on display in the Great Hall, celebrating the fact that the first pineapple to be cultivated in England was grown here in 1661.

Dorney Court is a member of the Historic Houses Association and can be visited on Bank Holiday Mondays and the preceding Sundays in May and every afternoon except Saturdays in August. For current opening times please check the Dorney Court web site (www.dorneycourt.co.uk). Adjacent to the house is a Norman church, the nearby village and garden centre, all of which are worth a visit.

The building is a great favourite with television and film crews, probably not just due to its looks but also the proximity to film studios and motorways, so it is no surprise that *Midsomer Murders* has made use of this historical location several times already. The house has been given no less than three different names in the course of the series. It became the Fox and Goose Hotel in the early episode *Strangler's Wood*, Bantling Hall in *Bantling Boy* and then, more recently, Allenby House in *Secrets and Spies*.

Interestingly, Barnaby hasn't been the only detective to grace this manor house and surrounding area: Hercule Poirot spent some time there in *Sad Cypress*, Miss Marple in the 2006 version of *The Sittaford Mystery*, Inspector Morse came here three times (*The Dead of Jericho*, *The Silent World of Nicholas Quinn* and *The Service of All the Dead*), while his former partner, Sergeant (thankfully now promoted to Inspector) Lewis visited in *Expiation*, and finally the 2000 version of *Randall & Hopkirk (deceased)* had scenes set here, too.

ENGLEFIELD - ENGLEFIELD HOUSE
ENGLEFIELD CHURCH

The Englefield Estate today covers some fourteen thousand acres in Berkshire and neighbouring North Hampshire, comprising farmland, forestry, residential and commercial property. A house on this site is recorded in the Domesday book, and the origins date back to at least Norman times. The name Englefield means either 'English field' or 'warning beacon field', probably relating to a big battle that took place locally in 870 between the Anglo-Saxons and the Danes.

The visitor approaches the main house though the model estate village built in the late 19th century, passing the church and rectory. It is a late Elizabethan E-plan house and was even painted in 1832 by John Constable. It has, however, been remodelled and refaced during the 18th and 19th centuries, without losing its main design. It stands in seven acres of mature gardens, some of which is a dedicated childrens' garden, some a walled kitchen garden, as well as a deer park. Queen Elizabeth I took possession of the estate in 1589, after the Catholic owners became involved in the Throckmorton plot and granted it to her spymaster, Sir Francis Walsingham. Today's owners, the Benyon family, over four hundred years on, are indirectly descended from him. It is a private residence, but open to the public by appointment for groups only, while the gardens are open to the public on certain days.

The *Midsomer Murders* crew used Englefield House, mainly the library and patio, in *The Magician's Nephew* as the home of Simon and Aloysius. Englefield church is attended by Aloysius in the same episode.

Other television credits for the house include *Inspector Morse* in the episode *Twilight of the Gods* and even Hercule Poirot, in the guise of David Suchet, has visited.

[Englefield House from the side]

HURLEY - CLOISTERS AND REFRECTORY
VILLAGE SHOP
YE OLDE BELL HOTEL

[Ye Olde Bell Hotel]

The Hurley area has been inhabited since the Bronze Age, and there is even a record of a village church in the Domesday book. Today, the village is a magnet for ramblers, fishing clubs and tourists all year round. Hurley High Street leads down to the banks of the River Thames and the weir at Hurley Lock, a popular place for freestyle kayaking.

This part of the River Thames is also widely used for mooring barges and boats making it a very picturesque spot. The High Street itself is a haven of listed buildings, including three 17th century almshouses. Around two miles away, in Burchetts Green, the old manor estate, Hall Place, now houses the Berkshire College of Agriculture, which has got excellent equestrian competition facilities for dressage, show jumping and eventing within its extensive grounds.

The Cloisters and Refectory were used as Dr. Clive Warnford's house in the episode *Blue Herrings*, with the adjoining Church of St. Mary the Virgin also in view. The monks' dormitories can be identified by the blocked up windows and doors.

Joyce goes to the pretty village shop to buy some charcoal in *Midsomer Life*, and Ye Olde Bell Hotel is used as the Magna Hotel in *They Seek Him Here*. Originally built in 1187 as the guesthouse of Hurley Priory, Ye Olde Bell Hotel sits in the centre of the village opposite the car park. David Suchet, in his detective guise of Hercule Poirot, also paid a visit here.

Other films shot in the area include *From Russia with Love* in which James Bond and Sylvia Trench have a picnic by the river, and the *Doctor Who* episode *The Visitation*, with Peter Davidson as the Doctor, which was filmed at the Tithe Barn.

LITTLEWICK GREEN - VILLAGE HALL & GREEN

This village lies just two miles west of the large town of Maidenhead in Berkshire, but is so secluded it is hard to believe that such a busy area is close by. The village comprises of a number of attractive cottages and houses centred round a large green, an ideal spot for film crews to work undisturbed. Littlewick Green originates from before the Norman Conquest, and some of its buildings date back to the 15th century.

Its most renowned resident was the Welsh composer, singer and actor, Ivor Novello (real name David Ivor Davies, 1893-1951). He lived at Redroofs, on the corner of the green, where many of his most famous works were composed. Many of his compositions were first tested in the village hall prior to transferring to London's West End.

This village hall, overlooking the green, was built in 1911, and has an interesting balcony, which doubles as both a scoreboard and viewing area for local and visiting cricket teams. The *Midsomer Murders* crew used this building in its original function in *Dead Man's 11*, and again in *A Talent for Life*, this time turning it into an antique shop. The village green was the scene for the cricket matches and a grisly murder in *Dead Man's 11*.

[The Village Hall]

One of the lovely thatched cottages was used as the Cooper's home, named Portland Place, which Tom and Joyce Barnaby considered buying during their house hunt in this episode. The cottage also appeared in *A Talent for Life,* along with several other houses for the residents of Midsomer Deverell in *The Animal Within*, with one of them taking on the role of the Mama Lucy Museum.

The village church is dedicated to St. John the Evangelist, and was consecrated only in 1893, after Littlewick Green had no church of its own for centuries. There was a private chapel in Ffiennes Manor (on the site of the present Ffiennes Farm), but its use ceased before Elizabeth I's reign.

The Old Shire Horse Centre nearby on the Bath Road is an added family attraction (www.theoldshirehorsecentre.com). The centre presently includes an animal farm, toy museum and craft village. It was originally used for exhibiting Shire horses, the gentle giants of the horse world, as its name indicates. Subsequently it was owned by a company supplying stunt horses to the film industry, and for entertainment through medieval jousting shows. The neighbouring public house, The Shire Horse Inn, was originally a coaching inn named The Coach & Horses, and retains many of its period features such as the low-beamed ceilings and fireplaces.

WINDSOR & ETON - RACE COURSE
LONG WALK
ETON BRIDGE
ETON HIGH STREET

Causton's race track, seen in the episode *Bantling Boy*, is actually the famous race course at Windsor, which is under the patronage of the Royal Family. The first race took place on the course in 1866. Later its existence was in doubt after bookmakers refused bets due to Winston Churchill's introduction of a betting tax, but this new burden was quickly abolished in 1926. In fact, 1949 saw Churchill himself amongst the race spectators, watching his horse, Colonist II, speed to victory in the Lime Tree Stakes.

Nowadays, Charity Events and prestigious Monday night race meetings are held at the course throughout the year, attracting many celebrities (www.windsor-racecourse.co.uk). Unfortunately, the successful horse Bantling Boy only exists in the world of *Midsomer Murders*, so no bets can be placed on him!

Of course, the town has not escaped Barnaby's attentions either. The road leading up to the entrance to the Long Walk was covered in choirboys in *Death in Chorus*. One of the imposing houses was also used as Francis Crawford's house in the same episode.

Windsor Castle is the official residence of Her Majesty the Queen. With a history spanning almost one thousand years years, the Castle sits in an area of around thirteen acres. Visitors from all over the world flock to see the famous State Apartments, the Drawing Gallery, St. George's Chapel and the enchanting Queen Mary's Dolls House. Other things to enjoy in the area include boat trips on the River Thames, walking and bus tours and, of course, shopping!

The bridge between Eton and Windsor became a location in *The Magician's Nephew*. Barnaby and Jones are seen walking over the bridge after leaving Causton Magistrates Court – which is in reality part of a nearby hotel. Actually one of the first cast iron bridges in the country, it opened as a toll bridge in 1823. The constant stream and weight of traffic on the construction forced it to be closed to motor vehicles in 1970. However, after a complete renovation the bridge was re-opened, for pedestrian use only, by Her Majesty Queen Elizabeth in 2002, her golden jubilee year.

[The bridge linking Eton High (left) Street and Windsor (right)]

In the High Street, Hugo Cartwright is seen leaving The George Inn in a drunken stupor and Eton Antique Bookshop becomes Hugo's Bookshop. This historic street also becomes the location for Anthony Prideaux's Antique Shop in *The Black Book*.

The High Street is home to some interesting buildings, some of which date back to the 1500s. The famous Eton College, founded in 1440 during the reign of Henry VI, stands at the end of the road, and can be viewed by visitors from April - September.

MIDSOMER COUNTY OF BUCKINGHAMSHIRE

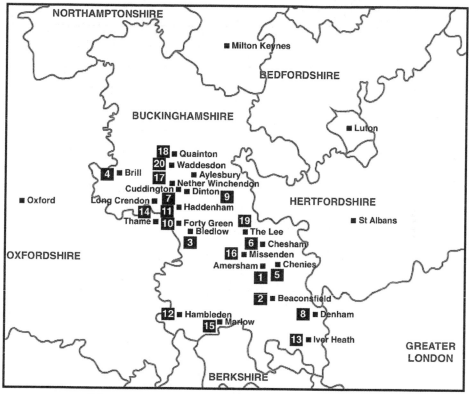

[Map of the Midsomer County of Buckinghamshire]

Key to Symbols

	Building (large or important)		Building (general place or structure)		Church (religious establishment)
	Hotel/Pub or Restaurant		Library		Market Square
	Museum/ Attraction		Preserved Railway		Shop
	Village Green		Village Hall		Windmill

Key to Map

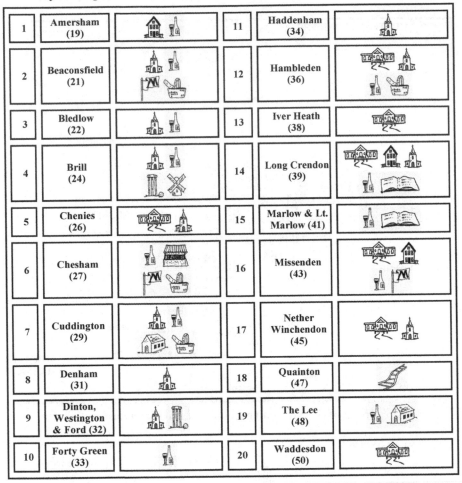

1	Amersham (19)		11	Haddenham (34)	
2	Beaconsfield (21)		12	Hambleden (36)	
3	Bledlow (22)		13	Iver Heath (38)	
4	Brill (24)		14	Long Crendon (39)	
5	Chenies (26)		15	Marlow & Lt. Marlow (41)	
6	Chesham (27)		16	Missenden (43)	
7	Cuddington (29)		17	Nether Winchendon (45)	
8	Denham (31)		18	Quainton (47)	
9	Dinton, Westington & Ford (32)		19	The Lee (48)	
10	Forty Green (33)		20	Waddesdon (50)	

AMERSHAM - POLICE STATION
THE CROWN HOTEL
MARKET HALL
THE MALTINGS

Amersham is actually split into two areas, the Old Town and the more modern area known as Amersham on the Hill. Both parts of Amersham have been a draw for the small screen.

In Amersham on the Hill the *Midsomer Murders* crew made use of the cells at the local police station in an early episode. Among other detectives that have paid a visit is Agatha Christie's Poirot, so expertly played by David Suchet. The town also has another claim to fame, a shop owned by Phillips Presentation Products, was responsible for producing the famous red books for the television series *This is Your Life*.

Amersham Old Town has been beautifully preserved and is much the same as it was in the 17th and 18th centuries. However, it has undergone some name changes through the ages, having previously been known as both Agmodesham and Elmodesham.

High Street in the Old Town has become a firm favourite, both with moviemakers and television crews, and especially The Crown Hotel which, although rebuilt in the 19th century, still sports some original 16th century features.

[The Crown Hotel]

These include a wall painting of Queen Elizabeth I's royal coat of arms, to commemorate her visit. King George III even made an unexpected stop here, asking for a carriage to Windsor and taking a drink before going on with his journey. Nobody actually realised they had been honoured with a royal visit until the King had left the hotel!

Its *olde worlde* charm has enticed many a production company into the area, but perhaps the best-known production to use The Crown Hotel as a location is *Four Weddings and a Funeral* (not to be confused with *Four Funerals and a Wedding* in Midsomer county!) for its famous four-poster bed scene. This hit movie starred Hugh Grant and Rowan Atkinson amongst others. The *Midsomer Murders* crew also took a trip to this hotel during the making of the episode *Who Killed Cock Robin?*.

The Market Hall, built in 1682, is seen in several *Midsomer Murders* scenes, being the focal point of the Old Town. The original market itself was held in the partially open space underneath the main building, with trade guild meetings taking place in the main room. The hall is still regularly used for various events.

Every year in September, the Old Town celebrates national Heritage Weekend by opening some of its historic buildings to the public. Entertainment includes guided walks, vintage cars being exhibited, Punch and Judy shows, Morris Dancing, and clowns. A town crier adds atmosphere. There are film and television location tours taking place, using an old bus, which of course do include some *Midsomer Murders* locations. Cream teas are usually offered in the Market Hall, and the Amersham band plays in the church gardens.

In 2008, St. Mary's churchyard played host to a special *Midsomer Murders Fete*. Bentley's Executive Producer, Brian True-May, was on hand himself to open the proceedings, bringing along Jane Wymark (Joyce Barnaby) and Laura Howard (Cully Barnaby) for assistance. A band played the *Midsomer Murders* theme, composed so skilfully by Jim Parker, whilst people could browse the bric-a-brac stalls, and there was even a very unique *Midsomer Murders* themed cake to be won in the raffle.

Midsomer Murders episodes filmed in the old town include *The Killings at Badger's Drift*, *Death of a Hollow Man*, *Death in Disguise*, *Blue Herrings*, *Dead Man's 11* and also *Sauce for the Goose*.

For example, The Maltings, around the back of the High Street, was used for the exterior shots of the Plummers' factory in *Sauce for the Goose*. The buildings, part of a brewery in earlier times, are now occupied by craft workshops and other small businesses. During World War II, local women actually made barrage balloons here.

BEACONSFIELD - THE OLD TEA HOUSE
ST. MARY'S &
ALL SAINTS CHURCH
OLD RECTORY
BURKES PARADE
BEKONSCOT MODEL VILLAGE

The name Beaconsfield is actually a corruption of Bekensfield, meaning a 'clearing in the Beeches'. Being conveniently situated close to the M40 motorway and having a mainline railway service to London as well, the area has become a sought-after place to live, and with so many fascinating buildings and history is also a great favourite with film crews. Like Amersham it is split up into two parts, the Old Town and the New Town.

Walking through the Old Town feels like stepping back in time. With so many listed buildings, it is almost completely unspoilt. Several of these 17th and 18th century buildings have been turned into banks, estate agents and solicitors premises during the run of *Midsomer Murders*. Being placed midway between London and Oxford made the Old Town an ideal stopping place *en-route* for horse-drawn coaches. There are still many signs of these enchanting old coaching inns and hostelries to be found today. Interestingly, it comprises of four sections of road known as 'ends' – Aylesbury End, London End, Windsor End and Wycombe End – it is where the coach routes from these destinations met.

[A quintessential tea house]

Just opposite the church in Windsor End is an enticing old-fashioned tea house in which Barnaby meets Miss Richards in *Blue Herrings*. Our hero wouldn't have had too far to travel in more recent times, as a building just down the road from the tea house was used in series eleven as the *Midsomer Constabulary*.

St. Mary's & All Saints church at Windsor End became St. Mary at Plea in the episode *Four Funerals and a Wedding*, whilst Barnaby and Scott also inspected a grave here in *Ghosts of Christmas Past*. Finally, the Old Rectory became Bouncing Barbara's office in *Written in Blood*. The church comprises of flint and bath stone. Its oldest remaining part, the tower, was built in the 15th century with the rest of the building being restored in 1879. The poet Edward Waller is buried in a tomb in the churchyard.

Beaconsfield's New Town has also proved a draw for all things *Midsomer Murders*. Joyce and Cully memorably take Barnaby to a rather trendy men's clothes shop (in reality both for ladies and gentlemen) in Burkes Parade to buy some new trousers in *Blood Will Out*. Barnaby and Jones also bump into Tristan Balliol at Jungs café in *The Magician's Nephew*.

Benjamin Disraeli was the First Earl of Beaconsfield, and one of the town's famous residents was the children's novelist Enid Blyton. She lived at a house named Green Hedges from 1938 until her death in 1968. Unfortunately the house has been demolished to make way for newer properties. However, you are able to see a detailed miniature version at the Bekonscot model village (www.bekonscot.com) which can be seen in *Small Mercies*. Reputed to be the oldest model village in the world, it is situated in the heart of the New Town. The whole of this fascinating attraction is set in the 1930s. Children and adults alike can enjoy and discover the secrets of the miniature landscape of villages, buildings, farms, castles, churches, woods, fields and countryside. There is also a miniature model railway running throughout the entire attraction along with a short narrow gauge railway on which visitors may ride.

BLEDLOW - HOLY TRINITY CHURCH
THE LIONS AT BLEDLOW

The Chilterns village of Bledlow is situated on the border between Buckinghamshire and Oxfordshire, and also on the Icknield Way, which is of Roman origin and nestling in front of Wainhill, whose name is Anglo-Saxon in origin and translates as 'Bledda's burial mound'. In the 10th century the village was recorded as Bleddanhloew and in the Domesday book as Bledelai. Above the village, carved into the chalk of a hill is a large cross. The theory is that this may be the barrow, or burial mound, referred to in the village name. Several local springs form a small pool called the Lyde. For many years the brook running from the pool into the nearby valley called the Lyde Brook provided water power for two local mills.

Church End in Bledlow is a conservation area with many interesting buildings. The parish church, dedicated to the Holy Trinity, was built mainly during the 12th and 13th centuries, and remains largely unaltered. The south porch has the oldest operational strap hinged doors in Buckinghamshire. Four steep steps descend to the nave, which is dominated by six massive pillars dating from 1200, each with a different foliage pattern at the top. If you visit look out for the Norman font in the Aylesbury style, and the recently conserved Medieval wall paintings and 16th century texts. The windows also contain some very good Victorian stained glass. The church appeared most notably in *Death's Shadow*, which starred Richard Briers as the resident revenge-seeking vicar. It also appeared in *Worm in the Bud*.

[Church of the Holy Trinity]

The gate to the right of the spacious churchyard leads to Lyle Garden, a fascinating water garden that uses some of the aforementioned springs. Owned by former cabinet minister, Lord Carrington, the garden is open daily free of charge.

Well-known, and absolutely worth a visit, is the local public house, The Lions at Bledlow, which is 16th century in origin, formerly consisting of three separate cottages. This creates a beamed interior with several inglenook fireplaces that ooze history. There are several rooms to choose from; a large main bar, a games room, a restaurant and seating outside to the front and back of the building. This public house is particularly popular on pleasant summer days.

The church, village and public house have been utilised extensively by a whole host of film companies, and *Midsomer Murders* has to date used this village no less than eight times. Other productions include *Miss Marple* and *The Four Feathers*.

In *Dead Man's Eleven*, The Lions at Bledlow changed its name to The Queens' Arms, and again in *King's Crystal* to The Dog & Partridge. It has also appeared in *Blue Herrings, Dark Autumn* and *The House in the Woods*. Other parts of the village can be seen in *The Killings at Badger's Drift, A Worm in the Bud* and *Birds of Prey*.

BRILL - BRILL WINDMILL,
ALL SAINTS CHURCH
VILLAGE GREEN
RED LION PUBLIC HOUSE
ROSLYN CHAPEL

Brill is located on top of a steep hill, and it is no surprise to find that its name derives from the meaning of 'hill' – Brill is a modern abbreviation of *Brey-hyll,* both syllables of which mean 'hill' – the first part originates from the Celtic language, the second from the Anglo-Saxon. This also gives a clue to the long history of the village, it can boast to be the site of an Iron-Age fort and a Roman lookout station. It also had a royal manor during its Anglo-Saxon period and was a place of strategic importance for Roundheads and Royalists alike during the Civil War.

Brill windmill is visible from afar, this post-mill (i.e. one in which the whole structure revolves around a central post in order to face the wind), dating from around 1680, is the last remaining structure of its kind near Brill. Since the 13th century windmills have been a feature of this picturesque village. It isn't quite the oldest windmill in England, but it is definitely one of the best preserved of the remaining dozen or so 17th century post-mills still standing. Brill windmill is open to the public on the first Sunday of each month throughout the summer.

Today's unusual common surrounding the windmill is the result of hand digging for clay for the production of Brill bricks and pottery, the two important local industries. Many of Brills houses still standing today are indeed built with Brill bricks, the last of which were produced in 1926.

Brill Windmill was used as Sarah Proudie's Lower Warden home in *A Tale of Two Hamlets*. Interestingly Watlington in Oxfordshire, around twelve miles away, was also used as a location for Lower Warden while some of the Upper Warden scenes were filmed in Lewknor, Oxfordshire, with a private house in yet another county being used for Upper Warden Manor. This being *Midsomer Murders*, Lower Warden is actually on top of a hill while Upper Warden is at the bottom, as Troy learns in the course of the investigation!

[Setting up for filming on the village green]

In *Four Funerals and a Wedding,* the All Saints Church was used, along with the large village green, which became the setting for the 'Skimmington Ride', based on a medieval ritual used to express moral outrage at a hen-pecked man, though women were also targets. Soup ladles are thought to have been used by angry wives to beat their husbands! Noise also played an important part in the proceedings hence the shouting by the crowd in this episode. The ones deemed guilty were often seated backwards on a donkey to express their foolishness. During the race seen in this episode, as Barnaby fires the starting pistol the vicar, the year's selected rider, is shot dead and falls from a mule. "Don't look at me," exclaims an astounded Barnaby to Jones.

The Red Lion public house was renamed The John Knox for *Four Funerals and a Wedding.* The interior was completely changed to make it look as if it was before the refurbishment it underwent a few years prior to filming, a bit of a *déjà-vu*! Finally, the Roslyn Chapel at the edge of the village green was renamed Pankhurst Hall (after Emmeline Pankhurst, leader of the British Suffragette movement) for this episode, the exterior being used as the incident centre during Barnaby's investigations, while the interior scenes were actually filmed at the village hall in Dorchester, Oxfordshire.

CHENIES - CHENIES MANOR HOUSE
ST. MICHAEL'S CHURCH

The focal point of Chenies village is the lovely Tudor manor house, which is quite distinctive due to its twenty-two individual cut brick chimneys. Formerly known as Chenies Palace, this Grade I listed building was originally owned by the Cheyne family who were granted manorial rights in 1180. The core of the present day structure was built by Sir John Cheyne around 1460 and later extended by John Russell (the 1st Earl of Bedford), remaining part of the Russell estate until 1950. Today the estate is owned by the MacLeod Matthews family, who are still working hard on restoration work.

The house has been graced by royalty on several occasions, with visitors including Henry VIII and Queen Elizabeth I. Not surprisingly, it is not without some ghostly visitations too! In the main house, strange footsteps are sometimes heard during the night around the central spiral staircase area.

The present day owners have created a beautiful garden that comprises various enchanting areas including sunken, rose, physic and kitchen gardens as well as a yew maze, in which visitors can lose themselves. These lovely areas also have two distinct plantings for spring and summer.

[Side view of Chenies Manor House]

The Manor first appeared in *Midsomer Murders* when it became the home of the rather reticent actor Edward Allardice, whom Cully goes to interview in *Judgement Day*. The exterior later became the Aspern Hall

Museum and the scene of eerie goings-on in *Beyond the Grave*, though the interior shots were filmed elsewhere. The village green and Manor Lodge are also seen in the same episode.

Orchis Fatalis marks the last *Midsomer Murders* appearance of Chenies Manor House to date, with the building standing in for Malham Manor, and the grounds being used for the Midsomer Malham Annual Flower & Orchid Show.

Over the years, Chenies Manor House has attracted one or two other visitors from the filming world. The *Rosemary & Thyme* Christmas episode *The Cup of Silence*, the BBC series *Little Dorrit*, complete with a specially built gazebo, and even a Marks & Spencer Christmas television advert were all filmed here.

The Manor House and garden are open from April to October, Wednesdays, Thursdays and Bank Holiday Mondays from 14:00 – 17:00. There is also a tearoom and a gift shop as well as plants for sale.

St. Michael's Church lies adjacent to Chenies Manor and was used in *Beyond the Grave* as Aspern Tallow church, the location of more unexplained happenings. David Mackillop's grave was also in the churchyard. The church was originally built of flint in the 15th century. However, many changes and restoration work have taken place since. The attached Bedford Chapel contains John Russell's tomb and is reputed to be the richest parish church storehouse containing funeral monuments in the country.

CHESHAM - CHURCH STREET
MARKET SQUARE
HIGH STREET
CHESHAM BUILDING SOCIETY
GEORGE & DRAGON PUBLIC HOUSE
SWEET MEMORIES
CHESHAM MUSEUM

Chesham was known as *Ceasteleshamm* in Saxon times, meaning 'heap of stones by the watermeadow'. The Meades Water Gardens in the old quarter used to house a watercress bed and three chalk streams merge here to form the start of the River Chess, hence its name. A riverside walk makes a pleasant distraction from the bustling town centre. The largest settlement in the Chilterns, Chesham, like neighbouring Amersham, has its own Metropolitan line station and so is easily accessible from London. The town is divided into two by the A416.

Church Street in the old quarter famously appeared in *Written in Blood*, where one of the houses became a bookshop. Barnaby and Troy were also seen driving past some of the charming old cottages. Until the beginning of the 19th century, Church Street was the main commercial hubbub of Chesham, housing a brewery, boot factory and numerous shops.

The 12th century Church of St. Mary's is tucked away behind the main street. Near the church is The Bury, an old Buckinghamshire town house that is occasionally open to the public. Market Square and the pedestrianised High Street stand in for Causton in *The Axeman Cometh*. In one scene, Jack 'Axeman' Mckinley roars down the High Street into Market Square in the wake of a trail of hippies. The town is promoting the forthcoming Midsomer Rocks Festival at Badger's Drift, which gets Barnaby uncharacteristically excited about seeing his musical youth idols – and in the course of the investigation, he gets to strum a guitar with 'Axeman'! The *Midsomer Murders* crew decorated the whole area with banners and market stalls to advertise the occasion. The Chesham Building Society, the oldest of its kind in England, was turned into The Causton Building Society for the filming, and The George and Dragon public house in the High Street also put in an appearance. Before the arrival of the railway, this old inn was used as the departure point for stagecoaches

[Filming in Chesham]

The Crystal Goddess shop (now Sweet Memories) in the Market Square retained its real name for *Things That Go Bump in the Night* and the former Chapter One bookshop (now Chesham Museum) next door was used in *Sins of Commission*, later being transformed into The Hogson Society headquarters in *The Black Book*. Finally, a building off the High Street became the dubious nightclub that Barnaby and Troy visit in *Written in Blood*.

Not yet visited by Barnaby (but give it time!), although most certainly worth exploring, is Lowndes Park. The Lowndes family donated this area to the town in 1953. It boasts a large pond with ducks and swans and a variety of trees and wildlife. Visitors may even catch a glimpse of a red kite, a bird that has seen a very successful breeding programme in the Chilterns.

CUDDINGTON - VILLAGE SHOP
ST. NICHOLAS CHURCH
THE CROWN PUBLIC HOUSE
VILLAGE HALL

This charming village lies mostly within a conservation area above the Nether Winchendon valley with the River Thame at its base. It has a population of about six hundred and has been a site of human settlement for centuries. Being very traditionally built, around the church and two village greens, if it is a glimpse of an olden days English village you're after, this is the place to visit. You'll find lots of thatched and whitewashed cottages, a traditional store-cum-Post Office (as seen in the episodes *Death of a Stranger* and *Talking to the Dead*, where it was turned into Paradorma, a spiritualist shop), and a picturesque village hall, all set amongst small winding lanes, right out of a picture guide book. Many houses and walls are made of wychert (the local name for earth walling built on a plinth of rubble and topped with tiles). This type of building material is unique to Cuddington and three other, adjacent villages in Buckinghamshire.

Cuddington has won several awards in the 'Best Kept Village' and 'Britain in Bloom' competitions, as well as honours for cleanliness and floral excellence. The *Midsomer Murders* film crew were drawn here for several episodes, namely *Death in Disguise*, *Death of a Stranger*, *Death and Dreams*, *Bad Tidings*, *Shot at Dawn* and *Talking to the Dead*. Other film productions have found this village to be ideal as a film set as well, including an ITV adaptation of *Oliver Twist*.

The ancient St. Nicholas Church has, through the ages, played a prominent role in the life of the village and this tradition continues today. There has been a church on this site since the late 11th century, but nothing remains of the original structure. Work on the current church commenced in 1220, taking almost a hundred years to complete with additions in both the 14th and 15th centuries. During Victorian times, in 1857, the church underwent extensive renovations and restoration, managed by George Edward Street, a well-known architect of that time. His work also includes the Law Courts in the Strand in London. In the 20th century, some additions and restorations were undertaken, but the character of the church today remains largely influenced by the Victorians. The eight bells, which give a full octave, are still very much in use, and the bell ringers can be heard practicing every Friday night.

The churchyard became a *Midsomer Murders* location in *Shot at Dawn*, where Barnaby visits the graves of Douglas Hammond and Thomas Hicks, the two war comrades who start the two families feuding in this story.

The Crown public house is essentially a traditional English country public house in a Grade II listed building, with rather low beamed dining areas, a locals' bar, and also a big inglenook fireplace. This lovely thatched building provided the *Midsomer Murders* crew with a charming backdrop in *Death in Disguise*, where Barnaby picks up Cully as she gets off a coach outside.

[The Crown public house]

Barnaby and Troy set up their incident centre in the village hall, a medieval structure, during their investigation in *Death of a Stranger*. It also made a reappearance in two further episodes – *Death and Dreams* where it became the bands' headquarters, and in *Bad Tidings* the scene for the Spanish evening, when the murder victim is found in true *Midsomer Murders* style, dressed in a Spanish flamenco costume with a red rose in her mouth!

The July village fete draws thousands of visitors each year and is recognised as one of the best in the county. In 2008, the event had a Victorian theme and also included a 'murder weapon' hunt. Hints to its location were given in a special issue of the local paper, *The Bucks Herald*. The 'murder weapon' was, in fact, a silver *Midsomer Murders* letter opener, and the lucky finder was allowed to keep it along with a bag of further *Midsomer Murders* goodies, kindly donated by Bentley Productions. The traditional entertainment on offer included Aunt Sally (a traditional Oxfordshire game played at public houses in the county and played in *Dark Autumn*), Punch and Judy shows, bar skittles and horse drawn wagon rides around the village lanes. Villagers strolling around in Victorian dress completed the authentic touch.

DENHAM - ST. MARY THE VIRGIN CHURCH

Denham village lies tucked away off the A40 in Buckinghamshire. Anglo Saxon in origin, the village name means 'homestead in a valley'. Remaining timeless with many historic buildings and quaint old public houses, it became the village of Draycott in *Ghosts of Christmas Past* with the church putting in an appearance in both *Death in Chorus* and *Blood Wedding*.

Among the impressive houses are Denham Court, lying close to the church and Denham Place, Sir Roger Hill's (High Sheriff of Buckinghamshire in 1673) residence at the end of the 17th century. Other old houses include Southlands Manor, Denham Mount and Maltmas Green.

Former residents have included Sir John Mills, Cilla Black, Sir Roger Moore, Mike Oldfield and co-Bond Producer Harry Saltzman.

[Denham Church]

The Church of St. Mary the Virgin has become a big draw for Barnaby and his team, perhaps because Executive Producer, Brian True-May and his wife, Maureen, were married here in 1969. With the exception of the tower, most of Denham church dates from the 15th century. There are numerous brasses and monuments, some dating from the 15th and 16th centuries.

Other items of interest include a 13th century purbeck marble font, a 15th century Doom painting over the south door and a bust of Sir Roger Hill of Denham Place. The Midsomer Worthy Choir sang here in *Death in Chorus* and Cully was married in the church in *Blood Wedding*.

In *Death in Chorus*, Connor Simpson finds a pig's heart pinned to the wall in his house. Interestingly there is a human heart buried under the church floor in Denham! Sir Robert Peckham, once Lord of Denham Manor and Privy Councillor to Queen Mary, has a mural stone dedicated to him. In his Will, he asked for his heart to be buried in his ancestors vault in the church.

Renowned actor Sir John Mills is buried in the churchyard, along with his wife, Mary. The lovely house they resided in is actually right next to the church and now has a blue plaque commemorating Sir John Mills on the wall.

Due to its proximity to Pinewood Studios and the famous Denham Film Studios, Denham has seen its share of filming activity. Other television productions filmed here include *The Avengers*, the original series of *Randall and Hopkirk (deceased)* and *Inspector Morse*.

DINTON, WESTINGTON & FORD -
ST. PETER & ST. PAUL'S CHURCH
WESTLINGTON GREEN

The village of Dinton lies quietly in the Vale of Aylesbury, with the tiny hamlet of Westlington residing right next to it. Blessed with the rarity of no through traffic, it is a wonderful place to escape, both for residents and visitors. Dinton's most famous resident was undoubtedly the so called Dinton Hermit.

Simon Mayne of Dinton Hall and Sir Richard Ingoldsby of Waldridge Manor were amongst those that signed Charles I's death warrant. John Bigg was their clerk at the time and it is rumoured that he was the King's hooded executioner. Legend has it that Bigg became increasingly remorseful after the execution and started to lead the life of a recluse, living in an underground cave in the village. Existing off local charity, his clothes and shoes were made up entirely of patches of leather and he kept three bottles attached to his belt for strong beer, small beer and milk. His shoes have even been preserved; one can be found in the Ashmolean Museum in Oxford, the other one is thought to be in Dinton Hall. There are several reminders of the hermit, both in the village and nearby Ford, where a small hotel, The Dinton Hermit, displays a sign depicting Bigg complete with an axe and skull in the corner of the picture.

St. Peter & St. Paul's Church in Dinton was used for the wedding at the end of *Who Killed Cock Robin?*. The foundations were laid in the early 13th century, and although the church didn't have any pews initially, the famous Tympanum (a semi-circular, decorated area over an arched entranceway) over the south door was already in place.

[St. Peter & Paul's Church]

By 1314, the church had been enlarged to its present size and by 1415 a tower had been added. Nestling next to the church is Dinton Hall. It is thought that this mansion was largely built in the 16th century. However, many changes have taken place since then, resulting in much of the original architecture being lost.

Midsomer Murders first visited the green at Westlington in *Who Killed Cock Robin?* where a body is found in a well. The pretty thatched cottages flank this lovely area, though you won't find the well here – it was brought in as a prop for the story. The green received a second visit in *Dead Letters*, where it became the scene of Midsomer Barton's so called 'Oak Apple Day' celebrations.

FORTY GREEN - THE ROYAL STANDARD OF ENGLAND PUBLIC HOUSE

Forty Green, near Beaconsfield is reputedly the home of one of England's oldest public houses. Therefore, it is no wonder that the *Midsomer Murders* crew were enticed to this location to do some filming for the series. Once known by the local West Saxons as *Se Scip*, meaning 'the ship', The Royal Standard of England public house lies tucked away in a tiny country lane. Legend has it that young Prince Charles hid away in the pub's priest hole whilst on his way to escaping to France in 1651, after the battle of Worcester.

After Charles II's restoration to the throne, the new king honoured the landlord for his support by agreeing to change the name from The Ship to The Royal Standard of England.

Although the landlord certainly served the Royalists well during the Civil War, a more amusing reason is also cited for the name change: it is believed that Charles II often met his mistresses in the rooms above, making the landlord believe his inn should be honoured with the new name!

In the early days, the alehouse was used as a meeting place for local villagers. The Saxons actually brewed ale on the site, making the hostelry an even more attractive prospect.

Not surprisingly, ghostly tales linked to this public house abound. When the place came under Parliamentary control in the 17th century, some violent soldiers staked a group of Cavalier's heads on pikes outside the door. Included amongst these was that of a twelve year old drummer boy, who is said to be still haunting the building today. Look out also for the ghost in the bar, an unfortunate traveller who was crushed to death by a speeding stagecoach.

At the beginning of the 18th century, the inn was rather different from the more salubrious place found in present times. Upstairs rooms were used for gambling, whoring and drinking large quantities of alcohol, so much so that the sign over the doorway still depicts the famous legend: 'Drunk for a penny, Dead drunk for two pennies, Clean straw for nothing'.

Unusually for *Midsomer Murders*, the crew's visitations have almost been rather more temperate than these turbulent affairs! In *Death in Chorus,* Barnaby and Joyce attempt to have a meal in the public house before Tom is called away, and later there is an altercation between Laurence Barker and Francis Crawford at the bar. *Blood Wedding* sees Jones meeting Cully for a heart to heart before her forthcoming wedding to Simon. Jones is also seen later being kissed by Sally Fielding outside. Other scenes include Simon and his friends having a quick drink here before the nuptials.

This wonderful old public house has also attracted filming for other productions. Recent movies include *Hot Fuzz* in 2007 and *The Boys are Back in Town* in 2008.

HADDENHAM - CHURCH END

Haddenham is a large village of about five thousand inhabitants. Situated in the Vale of Aylesbury, it derives its name from the Anglo-Saxon *Haedanham*, meaning 'Haeda's homestead', or *Haedingaham*, meaning 'home of the Hadding tribe'. This could indicate that it is linked to Haddenham in Cambridgeshire, home to the Hadding tribe – followers of Cuthwulf from Cottenham who marched south-west in 571. In the Domesday book it is listed as Hedreham, but already by 1142 it was known as Hedenham. The village had a Royal Charter as a market town between 1294 and 1301, but the rival market in Thame, only three miles away, won a lawsuit and the charter was lost. After the dissolution of monasteries, which included the local one, King Henry VIII took possession of the village and passed it onto his daughter, Queen Elizabeth the first.

Like nearby Cuddington, many of its buildings and walls are built from wychert, and the four village ponds were used to breed Aylesbury ducks. Today, breeding only takes place on the pond at Church End in front of the Norman parish Church of St. Mary the Virgin.

[Church End complete with church and duck pond]

This tranquil scene appeared in *Judgement Day* where it became Little Kirkbridge, one of the contenders in the 'Perfect Village Competition'. Parminters the Butchers, where Eleanor and Jane Macpherson go to buy sausages in *Birds of Prey*, is close by along with some of the lovely cottages also seen in this episode.

Haddenham is home to St. Tiggywinkle's, England's first wildlife hospital and animal welfare charity. As the name suggests, as well as caring for badgers, wild birds, foxes, reptiles and amphibians, the hospital houses over five hundred hedgehogs and the visitor's centre boasts the worlds' only Hedgehog Memorabilia Museum. The centre is well worth a visit if you have time (www.sttiggywinkles.org.uk).

The village even has its own industrial area and a small grass-strip airfield, as well as the Haddenham & Thame Parkway railway station, serving both the village and nearby Thame. This links the area to Marylebone in London, and Birmingham in the Midlands.

Haddenham has provided *Midsomer Murders* with locations for several episodes, and a number of other television programmes and films have also been in residence, including *The Great Muppet Caper* (1981) and *Rosemary & Thyme* (2003). For *Midsomer Murders* aficionados the list includes: *Judgement Day, Orchis Fatalis, A Talent for Life, Birds of Prey, The Maid in Splendour, Vixen's Run, Shot at Dawn, Things That Go Bump in the Night* and *Midsomer Life.*

HAMBLEDEN - POST OFFICE & STORES
ST. MARY'S CHURCH
STAG & HUNTSMAN
MILL AND LOCK

The well preserved village of Hambleden, about three miles from Henley-on-Thames, is actually the heart of the Hambleden Estate, which comprises some one thousand six hundred acres of mature beech woods, pastures and chalk valleys in the Chilterns. The name Hambleden originates from the Anglo-Saxon for 'crooked or undulating valley', and is listed in the Domesday book as Hanbledene. It became part of Martyr Warren in *Blood Will Out*. The camera pans over Hambleden in the opening scenes, when Orville leads his horse and Romany caravan into the village. The area around the church was also used extensively in this episode.

With brick and flint cottages topped with red tiles, a water pump and chestnut tree in the middle, visitors are often surprised to discover that this village is not in deepest rural England, but only forty miles from Central London. A visit to the quaint village Post Office and stores, which also featured in *Blood Will Out*, is a must; also the traditional country public house, The Stag & Huntsman Inn. This lovely old pub also featured in the romantic comedy series *As Time Goes By*, starring Dame Judi Dench and Geoffrey Palmer, with the couple sharing a kiss on a bench outside as the end titles rolled.

Hambleden Manor, mentioned as belonging to Queen Matilda in the Domesday book, has an impressive history. Today's Jacobean style building was built in 1603 of flint and stone. Charles I stayed overnight in 1646, while fleeing from Oxford. In 1932, the Manor was bought by the Right Honourable W. H. Smith MP, a descendant of the founder of the newspaper shop chain of the same name. Since 2007 the estate has been owned the Schwarzenbachs. Another notable resident is Phil Vickery, the England 2003 Rugby World Cup player.

St. Mary's Church dates from the 12th century, and includes an impressive 17th century memorial to Cope D'Oyley, his wife and ten children. It is built from local flint and chalk with stone dressings under an old tiled roof. The tower boasts eight bells, the oldest of which is one of the few pre-Reformation bells still in use, dating back to the 15th century. The church preserves and exhibits Lord Cardigan's sea chest from the Crimean War, for which he became famous during the ill-fated charge of the Light Brigade. The memorial outside the lynch gate appeared in *Blood Will Out*, and so did the church tower, which Barnaby and Troy climb up in the course of their investigation. Finally a field near the church was also used for both the 'travellers' camp and chariot race.

Unsurprisingly, this pretty village, and its surroundings, have often been used as a location by film crews and include *Chitty Chitty Bang Bang, Dance with a Stranger, 101 Dalmatians, Sleepy Hollow, Band of Brothers, A Village Affair, Poirot, Rosemary & Thyme, Down to Earth, The New Avengers* television series and *The Avengers* movie with Ralph Fiennes. The *olde worlde* Stag & Huntsman public house also notched up several appearances in *Midsomer Murders*, being used in *Who Killed Cock Robin?, Down Among the Dead Men* and *The Glitch*.

[Hambleden Mill and Lock]

Hambleden Mill and Lock, about a mile south from the village on the River Thames, appeared in two *Midsomer Murders* episodes, namely *The Animal Within* and *Strangler's Wood*. The first weir was built here in

1420, and today's pound lock dates back to 1773. It also featured in the novel *Three Men in a Boat*. In 1829, the first Oxford and Cambridge University boat race took place between Hambleden Lock and Henley Bridge and was won by Oxford in 14 minutes 30 seconds.

IVER HEATH - PINEWOOD STUDIOS

Although *Midsomer Murders* is filmed almost entirely on location, Pinewood Studios is the home of Bentley Productions, the company who makes the series. All post-production is carried out here, along with script read-through sessions and, of course, the intricate planning that is involved before filming on a new series commences.

[The Pinewood mansion – home of Bentley Productions]

However, sometimes the location team doesn't need to go very far for the perfect location. *The Axeman Cometh* made use of the Victorian mansion house at Pinewood Studios, using this as Priory Hall in the story. Built in a Georgian style, the entrance to this building was also turned into the Midsomer District Council's offices in *Country Matters*. This old mansion was originally a private residence, called Heatherden House, before being purchased by building tycoon Charles Boot and turned into an exclusive country club.

Boot subsequently changed the club's name to Pinewood, due to 'the number of trees that grew there'. However, his ultimate plan was to turn the estate into a film studio. His dream was finally realised on 30th September 1936 when the studios were officially opened by the Parliamentary Secretary to the Board of Trade.

The gardens around Heatherden Hall are also another big attraction for film makers and these have graced the screens in countless television series and films over the years. These formal gardens include a picturesque lake, fountain and bridge, making it an irresistible attraction for film crews.

Pinewood Studios is one of the Europe's leading film, television and media complexes. Plans have also been granted for redevelopment of the existing studio site to improve the facilities. The vision is headlined as 'Project Pinewood, the first purpose-built living and working community for film, television and the creative industries'.
Midsomer Murders is amongst elite company at Pinewood Studios. Some of the country's most famous films have used the facilities here. These include, of course, most of the *James Bond* movies, the *Harry Potter* series, *Slumdog Millionaire*, *Mamma Mia*, *The League of Gentlemen* and the *Carry On* series, to name but a few. Television productions include *New Tricks, Jonathan Creek, Little Dorrit, The Avengers, UFO* and the United Kingdom version of the quiz show, *The Weakest Link*, with host Anne Robinson.

LONG CRENDON - MANOR HOUSE
FROGMORE LANE
EIGHT BELLS PUBLIC HOUSE
CHURCH HOUSE
COURTHOUSE
HIGH STREET
LIBRARY

With the heart of the village full of thatched cottages, plus two manor houses and four public houses, the enchanting village of Long Crendon has proved irresistible to those involved in the making of *Midsomer Murders*. Lying close to Thame, another favourite for filming, Long Crendon was once home to the Earls of Buckingham. The village used to be a market town in the 13th century, though the market was later incorporated into the one in Thame. At one time, it was famous for being one of only two places in England to produce sewing needles, the other being Aylesbury (also in Buckinghamshire). In medieval times, Long Crendon was prosperous through lace and needle making, but the local cottage industry was destroyed by the industrial revolution in the 1830s.

The village has only been known as Long Crendon since the English Civil War, when the prefix 'Long' was added, in order to differentiate it from the nearby village of Grendon Underwood. Crendon is Anglo-Saxon and means 'Creoda's Hill'; it was listed in the Domesday book as Crededone.

Long Crendon has a small square, around which several local shops can be found. But the real treasure for visitors is the hidden High Street, where the picturesque thatched cottages and timber framed houses, some dating back to the 15th, 16th and 17th centuries, can be found.

The Tudor manor house, approached through an archway off Frogmore Lane, has fast become a favourite venue for some inventive moments in the world of *Midsomer Murders*. Seen in *Garden of Death* as the Inkpens' home, it hid some grisly findings in the garden, and the swimming pool later became a watery grave in *The Axeman Cometh*. The house again took on a different guise in *Things That Go Bump in the Night* as a spiritualist church. The original building dates back to the 15th century, with the west wing being rebuilt in the 17th century. Since then various changes and renovations have been carried out along with some extensive alterations.

Frogmore Lane has made several appearances in the series to date. Amongst these are in *A Tale of Two Hamlets*, where Barnaby is seen driving into Lower Warden and also in *Second Sight*, where he nearly runs over Little Mal Kirby.

Garden of Death used the Church House in the High Street as the location for the village hall, where the meeting about the future of the Garden of Remembrance took place. The exterior of the hall later became the Midsomer District Council Library in the episode *Blood Wedding*. The 16th century Eight Bells public house, also located in the High Street, appeared in the episode *A Tale of Two Hamlets*.

Dead Letters showed off the classic view of the church and Long Crendon Courthouse at the end of the village, additionally using the High Street for part of Midsomer Barton's 'Oak Apple Day' celebrations. The early 17th century Courthouse was used as manorial courts from Henry V to Victorian times. It is owned by the National Trust and can be visited between April and September. The manorial estate, in various expansions, has passed through the hands of the Crown, Oxford University, the Earls of March and is presently owned by the Marquis of Buckingham. The National Trust rescued the Courthouse from demolition. Indeed it was one of the first properties bought by the National Trust, and although the lower floor is still residential, the upper level can be visited. The entrance is via steep wooden steps leading directly from the street.

[Long Crendon Courthouse]

Long Crendon library doubled for Causton library in *Dead Letters*, with the interior also being used in *Blood Wedding*. *Death and Dreams* made use of the pretty High Street as well, and several of the lovely cottages served as various characters residences throughout the series. Finally, *The House in the Woods* has used Long Crendon for a scene or two, and most probably there will be more appearances throughout the run of *Midsomer Murders*.

MARLOW & LITTLE MARLOW -
TWO BREWERS PUBLIC HOUSE
LIBRARY
QUEENS HEAD PUBLIC HOUSE

The attractive town of Marlow is situated on the River Thames, and its name derives from the Anglo-Saxo language, meaning 'land remaining after the draining of a pool'. It was recorded as Merelafan in the Domesday book.

All Saints Parish Church, with its tall steeple, sits majestically on the bank of the river, with the town's striking weir and lock just up-stream.

This is undoubtedly one of the prettiest sights on the River Thames. Marlow, however, is doubly lucky in this respect: the present Marlow suspension bridge, built between 1829 and 1832, is also aesthetically very pleasing. It was designed by Tierney Clark, who also designed the Széchenyi Chain Bridge in Budapest (which was once the longest in the world). Plaques have been erected on the Marlow arches to commemorate the links between the two bridges.

The High Street has many old, interesting houses dating from the 16th, 17th and 18th centuries. Many of these have been sympathetically converted into shops. The renowned poet T. S. Elliot was once a resident in nearby No. 31 West Street from 1918-1919. Poet Percy Bysshe Shelley and his second wife Mary (author of Frankenstein) also lived in the same street, albeit a century earlier, from 1817-1818.

The town has seen a few visits by the *Midsomer Murders* crew. The Two Brewers public house, only a few minutes walk from the High Street, was used in *Sauce for the Goose*, for the scene in which Barnaby becomes rather enamoured with Helen Plummer over a drink, whilst Scott interrogates Caroline Plummer in the bar. Established in 1755, this public house is rumoured to have been the inn where Jerome K. Jerome wrote some parts of his novel *Three Men in a Boat*. The street outside and a neighbouring house can also be seen in *King's Crystal* and the local library stands in for Causton library in *The Black Book*.

Little Marlow lies three miles north-east of its bigger brother, on the former site of a Benedictine convent dedicated to the Virgin Mary. The convent belonged to Bisham Abbey, which is situated on the opposite side of the river to Marlow, but fell victim to the Dissolution of the Monasteries in 1547, and was demolished in 1740.

[**The Queens Head public house**]

The small village is tucked away off the Marlow Road and comes complete with a small village green, 14th century church, manor house and two public houses – The Kings Head and The Queens Head respectively.

Little Marlow became Morton Fendle in *Faithful unto Death* with several cottages, the 16th century Queens Head public house (exterior as well as interior shots) and village Church of St. John the Baptist all featuring. Barnaby and Troy are seen running and driving around the village green. Some of the cottages were also used in *Ring Out Your Dead, Tainted Fruit* and *Sauce for the Goose*, in which Derek and Dexter Lockwood live in a cottage on the High Street.

Inspector Morse also made use of the The Queens Head in his last episode, *The Remorseful Day*. The fact that the pub is located at the end of a cul-de-sac, allowing minimal disruptions for both locals and film crews, endears it to film producers probably as much as the good food it serves. Finally the local sewage works became a location in *Doctor Who*.

The village also has a special claim to pop fame, as 'Scary Spice' was married in St. John the Baptist church and had her wedding reception in the grounds of the local manor house.

MISSENDEN (GREAT AND LITTLE) - ROALD DAHL MUSEUM THE OLD POST OFFICE RED LION PUBLIC HOUSE MANOR HOUSE

The Buckinghamshire town of Great Missenden is situated in the valley of the River Misbourne in the Chiltern Hills, between Amersham and Wendover, not far away from the source of the river itself. It has a long curved High Street, with some wonderful half-timbered buildings and old coaching inns, including The George Inn, where visitors can still spend a night or two in low beamed rooms, and The Red Lion – now an estate agents.

The town used to be a prosperous stop along the coach route between London and the Midlands, but when the railway came and the coaches stopped operating, it became less important and more agricultural again. Church Street in the heart of the village also has a host of interesting old houses, and at its end, over the bridge spanning the by-pass, the 14th century parish Church of St. Peter & St. Paul can be reached. Its position in relation to the town itself indicates that the original settlement was clustered around the church and moved during the Middle Ages to its current location. In medieval times the settlement also boasted a monastery, which had been founded by Augustinian monks in 1133, but like so many, it fell victim to the Dissolution of the Monasteries. Its remains are today part of a Georgian mansion, which acts as a conference centre.

Great Missenden is well linked by rail to London, and is therefore a sought-after location for commuters, which is reflected in the local house prices.

The town featured in *Painted in Blood*, where the old National Westminster Bank premises were converted into The Shires Bank, which becomes the scene of an unusual bank robbery with Barnaby as an involuntary accomplice. This old building has since become part of the Roald Dahl Museum and a haven for children and adults alike who are fascinated with the writers' creations (www.roalddahlmuseum.org).

[Roald Dahl Museum]

Roald Dahl lived in Gypsy House, Great Missenden for thirty-six years, right up to his death in 1990, and is famous for stories including *Charlie & The Chocolate Factory* and *James & the Giant Peach*, both of which have been turned into successful films. He also wrote a series of short stories entitled *Tales of the Unexpected*, which were adapted for television. Roald Dahl is buried in the churchyard at St. Peter & St. Paul's Church.

Although not yet used in *Midsomer Murders*, the church is certainly worth investigating, especially during the summer months. Each Sunday cream teas and cakes are served inside, and at Christmas time a special charity service/concert is usually held here along with some amusing recitals by guest actors – these have included local resident Geoffrey Palmer as well as Pam Ferris, Roger Frost and Dame Judi Dench. Another famous former resident was Robert Louis Stevenson, author of *Treasure Island*.

Despite being a small village, Little Missenden plays host to an annual music festival that takes place in the autumn at St. John the Baptist

Church. This Saxon-cum-Norman building is worthy of a visit at other times too. Among the features of interest are 13th century wall paintings of St. Christopher, the Crucifixion and a series of cartoons illustrating the life of St. Catherine. Little Missenden also has a wealth of pretty old cottages with some old mill buildings and a mill house near the end of the village.

Little Missenden is often thought to be the spiritual home of *Midsomer Murders*. One of the working titles for the series is reputed to have been *The Missenden Murders*. Situated only a short distance away from its bigger namesake, the village appeared in the first ever episode *The Killings at Badger's Drift*. One of the houses became the home of the notorious mother and son team, the Rainbirds, who spied on the residents for ill gain. However, you won't find the eyrie seen on top of the house; it was specially constructed for the programme! Another cottage, formerly The Old Post Office, was also used in the same episode.

The old 18th century Red Lion public house has also made one or two appearances. It was used in *Destroying Angel*, under its real name, but became The White Swan in *Who Killed Cock Robin?* and then The Monks Retreat in *Talking to the Dead*.

The local manor house stood in for Dr. Wellow's home in *Dead Letters,* and also the doctor's practice in *Death and Dust*. The building originates from the 16th century, with additions being made in both the 17th and 18th centuries. Local residences were also used in *Four Funerals and a Wedding* and *Picture of Innocence.*

NETHER WINCHENDON -
ST. NICHOLAS CHURCH
NETHER WINCHENDON HOUSE

The tiny village of Nether Winchendon, with only about one hundred and ninety inhabitants, is a delight to walk around, with both brightly coloured and traditional Chiltern brick and flint houses. It is situated in the Vale of Aylesbury, close to the county border between Buckinghamshire and Oxfordshire. Its name is Anglo-Saxon in origin, meaning 'hill at a bend', and in the Domesday book of 1086 it was recorded as Wincandone. To complete the picture there is also a lovely old Victorian post box sitting proudly on the green in the centre of the village.

The parish Church of St. Nicholas appeared in *Things That Go Bump in the Night*, with the dubious Ronald Burgess as the resident vicar. It stands at the foot of a steep hill adjoining the manor house, and is medieval in origin, as it dates back to the early 13th century, with alterations to the interior not being carried out until the 17th century. Thankfully it has been spared Victorian influences, keeping a charm that has seen few changes since the 1700s. The single-handed tower clock is an excellent example of an early 18th century piece of which only about 6 remain in the country today. It also has an 18th century interior with a wide gallery at the west end, stretching across the full width of the nave, and it is listed in Simon Jenkins book *England's Thousand Best Churches*.

Nether Winchendon House was, when Notley Abbey was still functional, a priory, with some parts dating back to the 12th century. It was bought in the 16th century by the Duke of Bedford, and turned into a grand manor house. Since then, it has remained in the family for over four hundred years, and is still a family home.

Formerly the home of Sir Francis Bernard, the last British Governor of Massachusetts Bay, it was altered in the late 18th century in the Strawberry Hill Gothic style. The house is now a member of the Historic Houses Association.

[Nether Winchendon House]

It is generally open to the public for guided tours during May and on August Bank Holiday Monday (www.netherwinchendonhouse.co.uk).

The house turns up in several guises in the world of *Midsomer Murders*. This lovely old medieval and Tudor building proved to be the perfect location for The Lodge of the Golden Windhorse in *Death in Disguise* Both the house (most notably the 16th century dining room) and the grounds were used extensively throughout this episode. It was also used as The Priory, Lynton Pargetter's home, in *Talking to the Dead* and is where Jones nearly meets a gruesome fate. Lastly, it played a smaller role in *Garden of Death*.

46

Television appearances haven't confined themselves to just Barnaby's world; among other claims to fame in this genre are *Forever Green* with John Alderton and Pauline Collins, *Inspector Morse* in the episode *Dead on Time*, the *Miss Marple* episode *Murder at the Vicarage* with Geraldine McEwan, and a story with another of Agatha Christie's detectives, *Tommy & Tuppence*. In the big screen world, credits include the James Bond film, *Tomorrow Never Dies*. Scenes were also recorded for *Bridget Jones' Diary II: The Edge of Reason*, and although these were taken out in the final cut, they can still be found as extras on the DVD release of the film.

QUAINTON - BUCKINGHAMSHIRE RAILWAY CENTRE

With around one thousand three hundred inhabitants, Quainton village lies in the Vale of Aylesbury, about five miles from Aylesbury's busy town centre. Many Quainton residents commute to London during the week, though a fair number also work in neighbouring towns, especially Aylesbury itself.

Its name is Old English in origin, meaning 'Queen's Estate' (*cwen tun*), which probably refers to the wife of Edward the Confessor, Edith. This sounds feasible as Edward had a palace at nearby Brill. Originally the village was called Quainton Malet, which referred to the Malet family who owned the local manor from 1066 to 1348. The family had associations with the Order of the Hospitallers, who are credited with both the rebuilding of the Church of St. Mary & the Holy Cross around 1340, and the erection of the preaching cross on the village green. The shaft and base of the cross still remain there to this day. Many of the half-timbered and thatched cottages, which the village is renowned for, can be found around the green.

An imposing windmill towers over the heart of the village. This huge structure, sixty-five feet high to the top of the brickwork and a further eight feet to the top of the dome, was built during 1830-1832 but sadly stood derelict for most of the 20th century. It is the tallest mill in Buckinghamshire and is a Grade I listed building. Its bricks were kilned in an adjacent field from local clay. Milling by wind was soon replaced by the installation of a steam engine, which was unfortunately removed for scrap during World War I. Milling then ceased until the full restoration in 1997, when, thanks to the efforts of the Quainton Windmill Society, it ground flour for the first time in over one hundred years. The slogan of the Society is 'Flour Power'! Amazingly, the current owner is a direct descendant of the original.

Close to Quainton is the Buckinghamshire Railway Centre, a working steam museum, which provides a step back in time to its visitors (www.bucksrailcentre.org). In 1968, The London Railway Preservation Society moved its modest collection to Quainton, eventually making the twenty-five acre site home to one of the largest private railway collections in the country. It also boasts an excellent, half-mile long, miniature steam railway – a delight to both children and adults alike.

The centre was used extensively in the *Midsomer Murders* episode *Things That Go Bump in the Night*. The old Quainton Road Station, immortalised in John Betjeman's poem *Metroland*, and now part of the museum, became Fletcher's Cross, scene of the village fete. Barnaby, Joyce, Cully and Scott enjoy a day out at the fete in this episode, with a visiting steam train mysteriously shrouding the medium, Rosetta Price. The old railway was also the passion of one of the episodes characters, James Griss, who devoted his life to restoring Fletcher's Cross station.

[An 0-6-0 saddle tank in full steam]

Viewers can also catch a glimpse of part of the museum in *Down Among the Dead Men,* when Barnaby and Jones await a possible suspect on the bridge that overlooks the railway centre.

THE LEE - COCK & RABBIT PUBLIC HOUSE VILLAGE GREEN

[The Cock & Rabbit public house]

This picturesque village is often thought of as the quintessential English village. Tucked away in the Chiltern countryside, the village green is surrounded by pretty cottages and also flanked by The Cock & Rabbit public house, often frequented by DCI Tom Barnaby in his quest for law and order. Visitors should look out for the large autographed photograph of Barnaby and Troy in the hallway. It was here in *Painted in Blood*, that an impressionable DS Troy has a drink with the two officers from the NCS when DCI Tom Barnaby, who is somewhat less impressed with the 'boys from the big city', turns up to talk to him while investigating Operation Pond Life.

Part of the village is still owned by the Liberty family. On the approach to the green a striking wooden figurehead of Admiral Lord Howe can be

49

seen at the gate of a house built by Arthur Liberty for his nephew, Ivor Stewart-Liberty. The ship head comes from an old Navy warship, the HMS Impregnable, that was dismantled in 1921. Another part of the ship was also used for the mock Tudor extension of the famous Liberty store in London's Regent Street.

Rather unusually, The Lee has two churches adjacent to one another. The newer church, St. John the Baptist, was built in 1867 next to an ancient chapel, known today as the Old Church. This actually dates from the early 13th century, but is built on even older foundations. It is a lovely example of the early English Gothic period and also boasts a rare 13th century glass window, as well as an unusual Puritan window depicting Oliver Cromwell. This window was placed here in 1902, after being rejected by Great Hampden Church, for which it was originally made. Also, this small church has wall paintings, the earliest dating from the 14th century, which have been restored as far as possible. During the summer months cream teas in the grounds provide a welcome respite for residents and ramblers alike, and the profits made go towards the upkeep of the Old Church. Step through the hedges and feel transported back into medieval times.

The village also boasts an annual fete, flower show and thriving Women's Institute. In fact, in 2003 John Nettles was star guest at the fete, opening the event, much to the delight of everyone in the community.

Former Blue Peter presenter John Craven was once a resident, while renowned actor Geoffrey Palmer has also lived here for many years.

The area around the local manor house, village green and old church is now a conservation area and many of the cottages are listed buildings. Of course, such a lovely environment has proved irresistible to film makers. On the *Midsomer Murders* front it has, to date, been seen in *The Killings at Badger's Drift, Death of a Hollow Man, Death's Shadow, Death of a Stranger, Painted in Blood* and *Death in a Chocolate Box* (where most notably the Bentley Productions prop department built a *Camera Obscura* on the village green). Other productions that have used the village include *The Mrs. Bradley Mysteries* with Diana Rigg, the 1999 television production of *Oliver Twist*, and the television series *Pie in the Sky*, with Richard Griffiths and Maggie Stead. Anneka Rice even dropped into The Lee via helicopter for the popular television game show *Treasure Hunt*.

WADDESDON - WADDESDON MANOR

To call Waddesdon Manor a country house is somewhat of an understatement – it is actually a neo-renaissance building in the style of a French chateau, as found in the Loire Valley, with a large estate around it. Ornate luxury comes to mind when looking at the magnificent large mansion, not a surprise considering that its owner was a member of the Rothschild banking dynasty. His chosen architect was Gabriel-Hippolyte Destailleur.

It may look old-fashioned on the outside, but on the inside, the Baron had the most modern innovations of the 19th century incorporated, for example a steel frame, which permits the layout of the upper floors to be totally different to that of the lower floors. It also has hot and cold running water in its bathrooms, central heating and an electric bell system as well as electric lighting. The Manor housed an extensive French 18th century collection of fine art as well as English and Dutch paintings, some of which were passed on to the British Museum as the 'Waddesdon Bequest' after the Baron died in 1898.

[Waddesdon Manor in bloom]

The gardens were landscaped extensively, under the guidance of the French landscape architect Lainé. Not a mean feat as the hilltop was barren, and several fully grown trees were planted, some so big it took sixteen horses to move them to their new location. It is regarded as one of the finest Victorian gardens in Britain. Queen Victoria invited herself to view the park, but is reported to have been more fascinated by the new invention of electric lighting that had been installed – it is said that she spent ten minutes switching a chandelier on and off. While some collections were bequeathed, following generations of Rothschilds have added to the fine art and furniture collections, and they continue to be a draw for visitors.

The grounds and property have been owned by the National Trust (www.waddesdon.org.uk) since 1957, but continue to be administered by a Rothschild family trust as a semi-independent operation, which is an unprecedented arrangement – normally the National Trust does that itself once it takes ownership of a property and former owners tend to be no longer involved. James de Rothschild bequeathed the Manor and its contents along with two hundred acres of grounds and the largest ever endowment to the National Trust – £750,000. Eythrope and the rest of the Waddesdon estate remain in the Rothschild family's possession. The Rothschilds tended to reside around the borders of Hertfordshire and Buckinghamshire, an area unofficially known as 'Rothschildshire', and at one point they owned seven large country houses and thirty thousand acres of land in the area, and further afield another forty great Rothschild properties across Europe. The current baron, Jacob Rothschild, 4th Lord Rothschild, has overseen a major restoration and introduced new collections.

On 10th June 2003, approximately one hundred, irreplaceable and priceless, French gold snuff boxes and bejewelled trifles were stolen, none of which has thus far been recovered. There is still a reward on offer for information leading to their recovery. Strangely enough, DCI Barnaby hasn't to date attempted to solve this crime!

He did, however, enjoy a meal with his family in the café, although in the scene, which was from the episode *Death of a Stranger*, it was purported that he is on holiday in France in a French restaurant! The grounds also made a brief appearance.

Other films that made use of the stunning house and gardens include, *Carry On Don't Lose Your Head, An Ideal Husband, Daniel Deronda, The Tenth Kingdom* and *The Queen* starring Dame Helen Mirren, where it stood in for Buckingham Palace gardens.

MIDSOMER COUNTY OF HERTFORDSHIRE

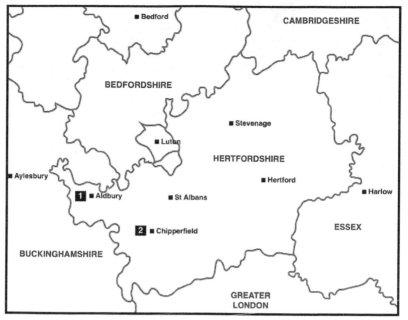

[Map of the Midsomer County of Hertfordshire]

Key to Symbols

	Building (general place or structure)		Hotel/Pub or Restaurant		Village Green

Key to Map

1	Aldbury (53)		2	Chipperfield (54)	

ALDBURY - VILLAGE GREEN

This picturesque village is definitely one of those quintessential English places with lots of charm and history. It is very popular with visitors and hence parking can be difficult, but be assured, the best way to explore this prime example of pastoral England is on foot.

[Laura Hutton's antique shop]

It is located in a valley at the foot of the Chilterns, about half a mile away from the extensive Ashridge Estate. The magnificent Ashridge House presides over a five thousand acre area containing woodland, common and chalk downland that supports a rich and varied wildlife. It was once home to Queen Elizabeth I and is now a world-renowned management training college. It does have a fully accessible visitor centre and a tearoom, and is today under the ownership of the National Trust. The estate's focal point is the monument, which was erected in 1832 to commemorate the Duke of Bridgewater.

Aldbury centres around its village green, which unusually includes a sizeable pond along with a well-preserved whipping-post and stocks. One main attraction in the centre of the village is certainly The Greyhound Inn, which for once has not been used by the *Midsomer Murders* crew (although Inspector Morse has drunk here). However, the public house has attracted one or two other television crews in the past. Aldbury became Little Storping in the Swuff in the *Avengers* episode *Murdersville* with Emma Peel (played by Diana Rigg) encountering some of the dubious villagers there.

In *Midsomer Murders*, one of the cottages was used as Laura Hutton's antique shop in *Written in Blood* and the title scenes were filmed around the pretty village pond. Other appearances include *The Shillingbury Tales, The Dirty Dozen, The Saint, Parting Shots, The Railway Children* (the 2000 version with Sir Richard Attenborough), *The Champions* and also *Bridget Jones: The Edge of Reason*.

CHIPPERFIELD - COMMON ROAD
THE WINDMILL PUBLIC HOUSE
OLD SWAN HOUSE

Although only a few miles away from Watford, the small village of Chipperfield seems like it is tucked away in the countryside. Luckily it still remains in the greenbelt and is completely unspoilt. Chipperfield used to be linked to the neighbouring village of Kings Langley. It is believed that the name is derived from the Anglo-Saxon word *ceapere*, meaning 'a trader', indicating that there used to be a market here in former times.

Unlike many of the *Midsomer Murders* villages today, Chipperfield still has a Post Office and general store in addition to a grocer, newsagent and butcher's shop. This along with four public houses and two garages make it an attractive place for visitors and residents alike.

Each summer, in true *Midsomer Murders* style, the residents open several of their gardens for charity as part of the Red Cross Open Gardens Scheme. There is also a weekend of Morris Dancing taking place on both the village green and in local public houses.

The common is a great attraction for ramblers. It comprises more than a hundred acres of woodland that includes a collection of sweet chestnuts. The oldest surviving tree is near the fish pool – and is over seven hundred and fifty years old.

[The Old Swan House]

Midsomer Murders makes its first visit to Chipperfield in *Written in Blood*, when Laura Hutton walks down Common Road and we hear her thinking about the lines for her forthcoming romantic novel. She passes both The Windmill public house, which is to be seen as the Calham Cross Inn in *Days of Misrule*, and also the cottage that becomes Linda Marquis's home in *Beyond the Grave*.

Barnaby and Troy visit a tearoom in the village, also in *Beyond the Grave*, though in reality you'd be hard put to find any refreshments at the location used, as it is actually a private house.

Nestling in a quiet close in the far reaches of the village is the pretty Old Swan House, used as Gerald Hadleigh's home in *Written in Blood*. It was originally constructed in the 17th century, subsequently altered and extended in the 18th century. In the 1800s it became The Swan public house, but has been a private residence since 1914. Brian and Sue Clapper's more traditional bungalow can also be found nearby.

Are you a fan of Midsomer Murders?

Then you should join the Midsomer Murders Society!

For more information and a membership application,
please send an email to info@midsomermurders.me.uk
or alternatively send a SAE to Midsomer Murders Society,
3 Rectory Court, Lewknor, Oxfordshire OX49 5TY, UK.

MIDSOMER COUNTY OF OXFORDSHIRE

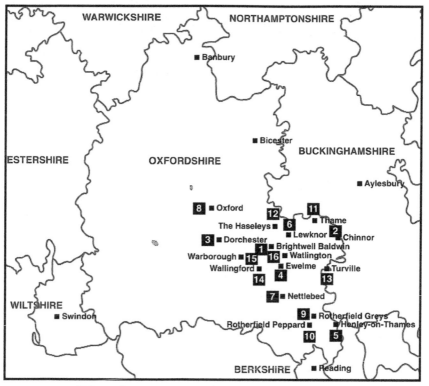

[Map of the Midsomer County of Oxfordshire]

Key to Symbols

	Building (large or important)		Building (general place or structure)		Church (religious establishment)
	Hotel/Pub or Restaurant		Library		Market Square
	Museum/Attraction		Natural Feature		Preserved Railway
	School		Shop		Village Green
	Village Hall				

Key to Map

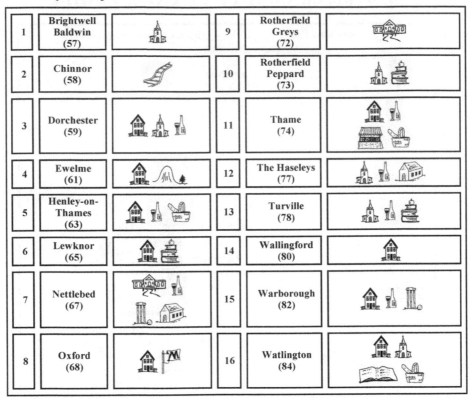

1	Brightwell Baldwin (57)		9	Rotherfield Greys (72)
2	Chinnor (58)		10	Rotherfield Peppard (73)
3	Dorchester (59)		11	Thame (74)
4	Ewelme (61)		12	The Haseleys (77)
5	Henley-on-Thames (63)		13	Turville (78)
6	Lewknor (65)		14	Wallingford (80)
7	Nettlebed (67)		15	Warborough (82)
8	Oxford (68)		16	Watlington (84)

BRIGHTWELL BALDWIN - ST. BARTHOLOMEW CHURCH

This small village, a spring-line settlement nestling at the base of the Chiltern escarpment, is located approximately two miles west of Watlington. Its name is a combination of Brightwell, which somewhat unsurprisingly means 'clear springs' in Old English, and Baldwin, which is taken from Baldwin de Bereford, who held three local manors in the 14th century. The oldest written historical evidence for a settlement is the Anglo-Saxon charter of 887. Of course, there are indications that there was a Romano-British settlement beforehand, not least the proximity to the Icknield Way, and the local springs that give the village its name very likely attracted settlers during the Bronze and Iron Ages.

[St. Bartholomew Church]

The village's main feature is the 14th century St. Bartholomew Church, together with Brightwell Park and the Lord Nelson Inn. Brightwell Park, behind the church, is actually the old servants' quarters to the original big house, that today lies in ruins and was in its prime twice the height (with a ballroom occupying the whole of the top floor).

The Lord Nelson Inn, opposite the church, is a traditional three hundred year old pub and was originally thatched. In the 18th century, gable ends and a veranda were added. It closed in 1905 and became a private house, but thankfully for current visitors, it is again a functioning public house. In 1971 a couple drove by, fell in love with it and decided to restore it. Today it sports a splendid inglenook fireplace and historic atmosphere, and in the summer the terraced garden, complete with weeping willow, invites visitors to stay.

Three *Midsomer Murders* episodes used this sleepy Oxfordshire village as a backdrop. In *Judgement Day*, a woman cycles through the village passing the church, while the church again features for the funeral scenes in both *Destroying Angel* and *A Talent for Life*. In the first instance the funeral party approached the church through the back gate. This is a favourite trick of the *Midsomer Murders* crew when reusing locations, since they tend to use different camera angles or approaches.

CHINNOR - CHINNOR & PRINCES RISBOROUGH RAILWAY

Chinnor lies at the foot of Chinnor Hill along the Icknield Way, which for centuries enjoyed a reputation for robbery, rape and murder (we're glad to report this has changed today – except for when the *Midsomer Murders* crew are around!), and is one of the largest villages in Oxfordshire with a population of about seven thousand people. There is archaeological evidence of permanent occupation from the 4th century B.C., however its name is Anglo-Saxon in origin from the 6th century A.D., when the village was called Siope(ora) of Ceonna. This became Ceonnore, then Chynor and finally Chinnor.

The village is documented in the Domesday book, and was a Roundhead troop station and battlefield during the English Civil War. A few 16th and 17th century houses still remain and many of the village's ghost stories and historical anecdotes date from this period. In more modern times, Chinnor is the birthplace of U2 rock musician Adam Clayton.

The area is one of the few in Britain that can boast a healthy Red Kite population. At the time of writing, there were approximately one hundred and thirty breeding pairs rearing around two hundred and forty chicks. The Red Kite is a magnificent bird of prey, with a reddish plumage, a distinctive forked tail and a five foot wingspan.

The Chinnor cement works, whose chimneys once were a landmark, and somewhat of an eyesore, in this beautiful area, have now been demolished. However, the striking chalk pit lake remains and has been used for filming, posing as a far away state in *Ultimate Force*, also a Bentley production.

[The train now arriving at Holm Lane Junction ...]

The main *Midsomer Murders* location though is the Chinnor & Princes Risborough Railway (www.chinnorrailway.co.uk), the station posing as Holm Lane Junction in *Death in a Chocolate Box*. Originally running a distance of eight miles, it opened in 1872, with stations at Chinnor and Aston Rowant, and level halts at Bledlow Bridge, Kingston Crossing, Lewknor Bridge and Wainhill Crossing – the latter also appearing in the same *Midsomer Murders* episode as the scene of a suicide. Due to low passenger numbers, the line closed in 1957 for passenger services, and finally in 1989 for British Rail commercial use. Maintenance of the branch from Chinnor to the junction with Thame, near Princes Risborough, was given to the volunteer-run Chinnor & Princes Risborough Railway Association from 1990, and passenger services resumed in 1994. Today the visitor can enjoy either diesel powered or steam train rides along this preserved line, with special themed days throughout the year.

DORCHESTER - ABBEY AND ABBEY MUSEUM
THE GEORGE HOTEL
THE WHITE HART HOTEL

This charming historic riverside village is only five miles from Wallingford, at the foot of the Sinodum Hills. Known locally as the Wittenham Clumps, the hills offer a wonderful panoramic view over most of Oxfordshire, and on clear days, well beyond the shire's boundaries. Despite its name, the river running through Dorchester is in fact the River Thame, a tributary to the River Thames. However, the two rivers join forces not far from the village.

The area shows traces of very early settlements, in the form of a Neolithic village fort, the remains of which are the Dyke Hills, situated between the two rivers. Dorchester was originally a Celtic market centre, becoming a Roman town (remains of which are under the allotments site today), and eventually an Anglo-Saxon settlement. However, it was Birinius, baptising pagan Saxon King Cynegils in 635 (when Dorchester was still called Dorcic and located in Wessex) for a political marriage deal, who helped to reintroduce Christianity into this part of England and turned Dorchester into a truly important location. Birinius was a missionary bishop and later, in 1225, was made a saint, henceforth being referred to as St. Birinius, and making Dorchester a popular place of pilgrimage in the process, as he was enshrined in the abbey. His baptism of Cynegils was a historic triumph, marking not only the first West Saxon bishopric but also the beginning of Christianity in the Royal House of Wessex, from which today's Royal Family traces its descent. When he arrived in Hampshire in 634 as a missionary on the orders of Pope Honorius I, he found the West Saxons 'completely heathen' and decided to stay in the area instead of heading further inland.

Dorchester today is a village of interesting and charming buildings, reflecting many architectural styles, which provide homes to about a thousand inhabitants. Away from the main street, there are lanes and paths to be explored that offer a sight of charming stone and thatched cottages. Many buildings in Dorchester date back to the 17th and 18th centuries, when it was an important stagecoach stop on the road from London to Oxford. This probably explains why there were no less than ten inns here during the 18th century.

The building of the Augustinian monastery began on top of older Saxon foundations in 1140. Today only the magnificent medieval abbey church remains of this structure which is still in use for worship and other events. The only other building that also dates back to the days of the monastery is the guesthouse which presently houses the abbey museum and a teashop.

The church has been extended several times, first between 1220 and 1230, again in 1293 when the north choir aisle was added, and in 1320, adding the south choir aisle housing the marble saints' shrine. Finally, the sanctuary was added around 1340. In 1536, the abbey was dissolved and the shrine destroyed during Henry VIII's reformation. The monastic parts of the church were bought by a wealthy local for use by the people of this parish, rescuing the abbey church for future generations in his time. Today much fundraising is done, not least by the American Friends, founded by Edith Stedman, who was even immortalised as a gargoyle on the outside for her efforts.

The abbey has outstanding examples of 13th and early 14th century glass windows and wall-paintings; medieval tiles; a Norman lead font dating back to 1170; a unique window combining tracery, sculpture and stained glass; and fine examples of Early English Gothic architecture as well as from the Decorated Gothic style. Visitors should not miss the Cloister Gallery, which opened in 2005, and take a trip through the abbey's architectural history. Visitors can also search for small remaining pagan signs, such as the Green Man carving in the south choir aisle.

Joyce Barnaby visits the abbey museum in the *Midsomer Murders* episode *The House in the Woods*, where it posed as the Midsomer Newton Museum and the nucleus of the local conservation group. This leads to Joyce's interest in the decaying 'Wynyard'. The abbey itself can be seen very briefly in *Four Funerals and a Wedding,* when Barnaby interviews the murdered vicar's 'boss', the bishop (played by Shaughan Seymour), who explains to him why the vicar became that year's rider in the 'Skimmington Ride' (see under Brill, Buckinghamshire).

The George Hotel is a beautiful and rare example of a real coaching inn, complete with oak beams and inglenook fireplaces in the hotel building. There is also a medieval guesthouse with a gallery around parts of the courtyard, off which some of the guest rooms are located.

It is, in fact, one of the oldest remaining inns in the country, having been built in 1495, when the stagecoach service from London to Oxford began. Situated right opposite the abbey and abbey museum, it appeared *incognito*, so to speak, as The Feathers in *The House in the Woods*. Part of The George Inn also became *The Maid in Splendour* in the episode of the same name.

[Entrance to The George Hotel]

The White Hart Hotel was built in 1691 and is larger than The George Hotel, incorporating a restaurant and a bar, with old oak beams and gorgeous old stone fireplaces. No two bedrooms are the same with some even boasting four-poster beds. The hotel can be glimpsed during some of the background shots in the series.

Other episodes that used locations in this charming village are *Things That Go Bump in the Night, Dead in the Water* and *Dance with the Dead*.

EWELME - RABBITS HILL
ALMSHOUSES
WATERCRESS BEDS

This straggling village, nestling in the Chilterns, is best known for its outstanding group of 15th century buildings, namely the church, school and almshouses, as well as its associations with Chaucer's granddaughter. Its name derives from *lawelme*, meaning 'a spring source', and it still feeds the cress-filled chalk stream running alongside the village's main road. On the hill above the village is the well-preserved church – it survived the Civil War through protection of the local Parliamentarian commander. Jerome K. Jerome, author of *Three Men in a Boat*, is buried here.

The watercress beds in Ewelme proved a thriving local business throughout the 20th century, supplying Covent Garden market amongst others. Present day regulations sadly prohibit the sale of watercress from this site and the industry has declined. Thankfully, The Chiltern Society has purchased the beds and has embarked upon a programme of conservation and restoration work. Special opening days and guided walks are arranged each month (www.ewelmewatercressbeds.org).

Visitors should look out for the almshouses and nearby school. The almshouses are reached from a covered walkway leading from the west door of the church. They are built from red brick and timber and are set in a quadrangle with a well in the centre, and encircled by a cloister walk. Although the school was founded as a grammar institute in 1437, it is now a church primary school and is the oldest of its kind in the country.

[Ewelme from Rabbits Hill]

For *Midsomer Murders* purposes, the whole village changed its name to Aspern Tallow in the episode *Beyond the Grave*. During the opening of the story Alan Bradford is seen showing a group of 'Jonathan Lowrie' aficionados the beautiful view of the village from the top of Rabbits Hill. He then takes them down to the almshouses in the centre of Ewelme – before rather worryingly ending up at Chenies in Buckinghamshire, which is over thirty miles away! The rest of Ewelme proves to be an enchanting backdrop to this story with the 15th century primary school and village houses all appearing on the screen.

The famous watercress beds are seen in the later episode *Secrets and Spies*. The production team again decided to capture the beauty of the view from Rabbits Hill in both this episode and *The Black Book*.

HENLEY-ON-THAMES - HENLEY BRIDGE
HART STREET
TOWN HALL
ARGYLL PUBLIC HOUSE
GABRIEL MACHIN

Best known for its annual Royal Regatta, which has been held since 1839, this market town with about ten thousand five hundred inhabitants is situated on one of the prettiest parts of the River Thames, about ten miles from Reading. Other successful annual events include the Henley Festival of Music & Arts and the Henley Food Festival. It is, somewhat unsurprising with its rowing heritage, home to the award-winning River and Rowing Museum (www.rrm.co.uk), which was opened in 1998 by Queen Elizabeth II and features a *Wind in the Willows* exhibition as well as information on the River Thames, the rowing sport, and Henley itself. Further attractions are the 15th century Chantry House, Mill Meadows park and the fourth oldest working playhouse in the country, the Kenton Theatre. There is also Asquith's Teddy Bear Shop, reputed to be one of the first of its kind worldwide.

The town's roots go back to 1179, when it was founded by Henry II as a river crossing and port for the supply of goods to London. The original crossing is only a short distance from current bridge that goes into the heart of Henley, with its historic church, town hall and market square. Although first mentioned in 1234, today's structure dates from 1786. Henley has good railway links into London Paddington and Reading, making it sought after by today's commuters as a place to live.

Dominating Henley's skyline is St. Mary the Virgin Church which has origins from about 1000, but the first documented presence dates from 1204, and the church itself is basically a 13th century building, although enlarged both in the 15th and 19th centuries. The present exterior is mostly Victorian, but the inside offers some fine examples of Early English and Perpendicular style. Worth seeing is the Great Mural on the chancel wall, designed in 1891 in the style of the Pre-Raphaelites.

In 1711 W. H. Brakspear, a distant relative of the only English Pope, Adrian IV, bought a brewery in Bell Street. The brewery moved in 1812 to New Street, where it remained until its brewing operations were sold in 2002 to the Wychwood Brewery in Witney. The building was sold and converted into a luxury hotel of the Hotel du Vin chain. *Midsomer Murders* may not have used the brewery for filming, but *Inspector Morse* did in the episode *The Sins of the Fathers*.

Famous people connected with Henley include Dusty Springfield, who has a gravesite and marker in the grounds of St. Mary the Virgin Church, although her ashes were scattered in Henley and at the cliffs of Moher in Ireland. Every year, her fans still gather in the town to celebrate 'Dusty Day' on the Sunday closest to her birthday (16th April). George Orwell spent some of his formative years in Henley and nearby Shiplake. George Harrison, the former Beatle, lived in a mansion called Friar Park from the 1970s until his death in 2001. Liam Gallagher (of the band Oasis) has a second home here. The former MP for Henley, Boris Johnson, became Mayor of London in 2008, while another high profile former MP for the constituency was Michael Heseltine.

Nearby are further attractions worth visiting such as Fawley Court, which was designed by Christopher Wren in 1684, with the interior remodelling by James Wyatt and landscaped gardens by Lancelot 'Capability' Brown; and Greenlands, formerly owned by W. H. Smith, but since 1945 home to the Henley Management College.

[The Town Hall]

Locations in this attractive market town have appeared in numerous *Midsomer Murders* episodes. In *Dead in the Water*, the well-known five arched Henley bridge can be seen and Barnaby and his wife come to town to see the regatta, having a picnic – when this scene was filmed in 2004, a gale force wind blew a gazebo across the setting narrowly missing the actors and hitting the director and some of the crew, but luckily nobody was injured. Barnaby and Jones visit a solicitor near the market square in *Down Among the Dead Men*, only just avoiding a parking ticket.

Later in the episode Barnaby buys Cully and her friends a drink at Cafe Vintners (which in real life is the tapas bar called La Bodega in Hart Street), while in *Last Year's Model* Henley becomes Causton, with the Town Hall exterior standing in for the Courthouse (other exterior and interior scenes being shot in Kingston-upon-Thames). The nearby Argyll public house hosted a meeting between Pru Plunkett, Barnaby and Jones in the same episode. *The Magician's Nephew* saw the traditional butchers in Market Square change its name from Gabriel Machin to Anton

Thorneycroft's Butchers, and finally the *Midsomer Murders* crew returned to Market Square for *The Black Book*, where the Town Hall became the Auction Rooms.

LEWKNOR - LEWKNOR CHURCH OF ENGLAND PRIMARY SCHOOL CHURCH FARM CHURCH LANE

Lewknor is a village nestling at the bottom of the Chilterns, just off the Ridgeway, an ancient long-distance track that follows the Chilterns east to west across Southern England. The name of the village is derived from *Leofecanora* meaning 'Leofeca's slope', while the 'nor' suffix means spring. The first documented reference to the village dates from 990, where it was referred to as Leofecan. In the area, remains of Bronze Age, early Iron Age and Anglo-Saxon burial grounds have been found, as well as proof that there was a Roman settlement.

In 1851, there were a dozen working farms in Lewknor, today only one of these remains. The original village shop and Post Office closed in 1999 after two hundred years of trading, and is now a private house. The Leathern Bottel, the only remaining public house in the village, is essentially a 16th-17th century timber framed building at the crossroads in the heart of the village.

The church, originally dedicated to St. Mary but later changed to St. Margaret, was founded in 1146. It is built of local flint with stone dressings, and was extended during both the end of the 12th and 14th centuries, while the last addition, the crenulated tower, was built in the 15th century. It shows some examples of late Norman work as well as Romanesque style. A small part of an original medieval stained glass window can be seen high up in the east wall of the north transept chapel, while further fragments have been worked into the tops of the chancel windows.

Lewknor Church of England Primary School was built in 1836, when the resident vicar persuaded the owners of most of the village at that time, All Souls College, Oxford, to buy some old cottages on the site in order to build the school. To this day, it retains many period features including a thatched roof and the old oak beams inside.

[Lewknor Primary School]

So far three *Midsomer Murders* episodes have used locations in the pretty village of Lewknor, namely *Death and Dust*, *The House in the Woods* and *A Tale of Two Hamlets*. In *The House in the Woods* scenes were filmed inside the infant classroom (before the recent extension) and outside the school, where the church was visible in the background. Mostly real Lewknor school pupils were used in the classroom shots, apart from the teacher and the boy who provides Barnaby and Jones with a clue to the case in the shape of a toy car. All participating pupils had special badges to cover the normal school logo on the uniform shirts. As filming took place during a half term break, the pupils had to come into school for an extra day, but none of them seemed to mind too much!

The school was also used in *A Tale of Two Hamlets*, where a bible quote appears overnight on one of the outside doors. The last remaining working farm in the village, Church Farm, was used in *House in the Woods* for a very brief scene. Finally, in *Death and Dust* a private house in Church Lane posed as Megan's cottage, where Barnaby and Jones interview Megan and her boyfriend after a doctor is killed.

NETTLEBED & CROCKER END - THE GREEN
WHITE HART HOTEL
VILLAGE HALL
JOYCE GROVE

Nettlebed lies on the Henley to Oxford road, making it an important stop-over for stage coaches in bygone days. Many members of royalty are rumoured to have stayed at the former Red Lion public house in the High Street. However, this interesting village is most famous for having an abundance of clay suitable for brick making. In the 13th century there was even a settlement of Flemish bricklayers in nearby Crocker End. There is still an 18th century kiln in Nettlebed that has subsequently been adapted for burning lime. Thankfully the kiln has been listed by English Heritage and is now under the responsibility of Oxford County Council Archives department.

Although it is not clear where the roots of the village name is derived, legend has it that it may have come from the fact that thread can be obtained from nettles and woven into linen cloth. In the 18th century many homes had bed linen and tablecloths made from nettles that are found in abundance in the area.

Both Nettlebed and Crocker End have been featured in *Midsomer Murders*. The large green and attractive cottages at Crocker End have been used in several episodes to date including *Judgement Day*, *The Maid in Splendour* and *Shot at Dawn*. The green at Crocker End became one of the locations for 'The Perfect Village' competition in *Judgement Day* and the scene of Midsomer Parva's celebrations in *Shot at Dawn,* when Tommy Hicks' name is added to the war memorial in the village.

Nettlebed itself appears in *The Maid in Splendour, Death and Dust, Dance with the Dead* and again in *The Magician's Nephew*. A small furniture and antiques shop became David Mostyn's Home Furnishings in *Death and Dust*.

The bistro at The White Hart Hotel in High Street appeared as the refurbished Maid in Splendour in the episode of the same name. Originally known as The George, the name was changed to The White Hart during the Tudor period. Henry VIII's favourite sport was hunting and a White Hart is a famous old English hunting symbol. It was also used as a billeting house for loyalist Cavalier troops during the English Civil War.

The inside of the village hall was used as the location for the dance school and 1940s evening in *Dance with the Dead*, with the both outside and inside being used for the fated magic show in *The Magician's Nephew*. Once known as The Working Men's Club, Nettlebed Village Hall was commissioned in 1912 by Robert Fleming and designed by the famed architect C. E. Mallows.

The large house known as Joyce Grove, now used as a Sue Ryder palliative care home, sits in its own grounds behind the High Street. It was used as Bledlow Hall, the opulent home of the Fitzroy family in *Blood Wedding*.

The house and village are famed for their connections with Ian Fleming, author of the *James Bond* novels. Ian Fleming was one of the grandchildren of Robert Fleming, who bought Joyce Grove, along with much of the village in 1903. Another famous family member was Ian Fleming's older brother, Peter Fleming. Peter became a renowned travel writer, marrying actress Celia Johnson of *Brief Encounter* fame in 1935. Current members of the Fleming family still live locally and remain involved in running the estate as well as taking an active part in village life.

[Joyce Grove]

Many of the family are also buried in Nettlebed churchyard including the aforementioned Peter Fleming and Dame Celia Johnson. The Sue Ryder home and its grounds also appeared in the Hercule Poirot episodes *Cat Among the Pigeons* and *Sad Cypress*, starring David Suchet.

OXFORD - BROAD STREET
THE ASHMOLEAN MUSEUM
BOTANIC GARDENS

The area of Oxford was first occupied in Saxon times, and was originally known as Oxenaforda, which means, somewhat unsurprisingly, 'Ford of the Ox', as it lies on the banks of not one, but two rivers – the Thames and the Cherwell. First mentioned in the Anglo-Saxon Chronicle of 912, it is today home to about one hundred and fifty thousand people.

This city is, of course, world famous for being home to the University of Oxford, which is the oldest university in the English-speaking world. The University consists of thirty-eight independent colleges and six permanent private halls. It has its origins in the 12th century, but the exact foundation date is unknown. Academics fleeing from a dispute between town and gown in 1209 founded the University in Cambridge, and a history of competition between the two ensued, which lasts to this day, as seen, for example, in the annual boat race. Both places are consistently ranked in the world's top ten universities. Oxford is home to a second university, Oxford Brookes University (formerly a polytechnic), which is somewhat younger since it was only given its charter in 1991.

The 'city of dreaming spires' (as coined by the poet Matthew Arnold) is known for other things too – it is the home of the Mini, an iconic car in the United Kingdom, and was home to the Morris Motor Company, the Bodleian Library, the John Radcliffe Hospital, the Ashmolean Museum, the fictional character Inspector Morse – indeed the list is almost endless. The visitor will find, as can be expected in a university city, many bookshops – the most famous of which, Blackwell's Books, claims the largest single room devoted to book sales in Europe. The city centre is relatively small, centring around Carfax, a crossroads forming the junction of Cornmarket Street, Queen Street, St. Aldate's and The High. Much of the centre is pedestrianised, and Oxford has several park-and-ride locations around the city ring road. A common sight in and around the city are dons and students alike on bicycles.

Midsomer Murder's first visit to Oxford was in *Who Killed Cock Robin?*. In the story, Melvyn Stockard's wife, Bubbles, has a jewellery shop in Broad Street called Bits & Baubles. The premises that were used were actually an artist materials shop called Broad Canvas. The building is Grade II listed and dates back to around 1700. Broad Street was originally where horses were traded in the 13th century, and also the place that the Protestant martyrs, Bishops Latimer and Ridley and Archbishop Cranmer, were burnt at the stake (with a cross in the road still marking the supposed spot). The street also houses the Museum of the History of Science, the Sheldonian Theatre (and the row of emperors' heads), several branches of Blackwell's Books, the New Bodleian Library as well as Trinity and Balliol Colleges.

Midsomer Murders returned to Oxford in *The Fisher King,* when Barnaby and Scott visit Dr. James Lavery at The Ashmolean Museum. The Museum is named after Elias Ashmole, a friend of the Tradescant family whose collection of rarities, known as Tradescant's Ark, was in the 17th century considered one of the best collections of its type in the world. In 1659, three years before his death, John Tradescant made over the collection to Ashmole by a deed of gift, but must have regretted this for in his will he stated that the collection should go to the university of either Cambridge or Oxford. Further, the collection was to remain the possession of John Tradescant's widow while she lived, and it was left up to her to decide which of the universities should receive the gift.

[The Ashmolean Museum]

Ashmole disputed the will for over ten years and even took a lease on the house next door to Mrs. Tradescant. The deciding factor was when it transpired that Mrs. Tradescant had been selling off pieces from the collection against her husband's wishes. Ashmole's claim was upheld and following an attempted burglary the collection was moved to Ashmole's house. Shortly afterwards Mrs. Tradescant was found drowned in her garden pond (maybe a cold case for DCI Barnaby?).

Ashmole gave the collection, including various items of his own, to the University of Oxford on condition that a suitable building be found in which to display the items. The first Ashmolean Museum was in Broad Street where much of the collection was neglected for most of the 18th century. However, by the 19th century the University also had other collections of a similar nature that it did not know how to display. A new Neo-Classical building in Beaumont Street, designed by Charles Robert Cockerell, was opened in 1845 and became the new Ashmolean Museum.

Today the Museum contains many noteworthy exhibits including the Alfred Jewel, Guy Fawkes's lantern, the Stradivari violin *Le Messie* and pictures by Holbein, Bellini, Titian, Van Dyke, Rubens, Rembrandt, Poussin, Gainsborough, Blake, Constable, Manet, Pissarro, Degas, van Gogh, Picasso and several Pre-Raphaelites.

Later the *Midsomer Murders* crew thought that the University of Oxford Botanic Garden would be the perfect location for the Orchid House, where Margaret Winstanley worked in *Orchis Fatalis*.

It was in 1621 that the Oxford Physic Garden was established by Henry Danvers, Earl of Danby, and was the oldest such garden after those of Pisa and Leyden. In 1840 it was renamed the Botanic Garden and today it boasts an alpine garden, a fernery, a grass garden, herbaceous borders, a water garden and a collection of historical roses. In the greenhouses are tropical plants, including bananas and rice, collections of ferns, succulents, orchids, insect-eating plants and water lilies. Notable firsts for the garden were the production of its own weed, the Oxford ragwort (*Senecio squalidus*) and the London plane (a hybrid of an Oriental and American species raised in 1665).

Danby had originally leased five acres of land from Magdalen College for his garden, which had formerly been a Jewish burial ground. First the ground had to be raised above the River Cherwell flood plain which took four thousand loads of 'mucke and dunge'. The gateway was built by Indigo Jones' master mason, Nicholas Stone, in 1632. An innkeeper, Jacob Bobart, who was also a competent gardener became the first Keeper in 1642. The job had been offered to John Tradescant, most associated with the Ashmolean Museum, who due to failing health had been unable to accept the post. Bobart was a good choice and produced the first catalogue of plants in 1648, by which time there were one thousand six hundred specimens.

Bobart's son succeeded his father as Keeper, and after Morison's death became Professor of Botany as well. It was Professor Daubeny, appointed in 1834, who changed the name of the garden and was the first to use it for experimental research. He also gave a party there for the victorious Darwinians after the famous debate between Huxley and Wilberforce over which he had presided at the Oxford British Association meeting in 1860. A garden outside the entrance, designed by Sylvia Crowe, now commemorates Oxford's wartime contribution to the science of antibiotics through the development of penicillin.

Normally an area for seasonal plant displays, special demonstrations and other events, the garden's conservatory was turned into an orchid haven for *Orchis Fatalis*. Although it was built to an original Victorian design in 1973, the conservatory is actually made of aluminium rather than wood and iron. Part of the gardens and glasshouses are also seen in the episode, particularly during the chase scenes at the end that also afford brief glimpses of Magdalen Bridge and the River Cherwell.

ROTHERFIELD GREYS - GREYS COURT

[Greys Court]

Situated on the edge of the Chilterns, just three miles from Henley, Greys Court is a picturesque Tudor manor house. Owned by the National Trust, it has 14th century fortifications, a beautiful courtyard, ornamental gardens with old-fashioned roses, a wisteria walk and maze, all set within its medieval walls. There is also a rare Tudor donkey wheel and remains of a medieval tower dating back to 1347. The house itself has some fascinating associations with Jacobean court intrigues. Greys Court sits in an estate comprising of two hundred and eighty acres, including formal gardens, woodland, parkland and common land.

Most of the estate falls into the Chilterns Area of Outstanding Natural Beauty. Despite being a National Trust Property, it is often one of the somewhat forgotten tourist attractions in Oxfordshire. Unfortunately, at the time of writing, the house is undergoing re-servicing and conservation work, and is expected to be closed until April 2010. However, the delightful gardens, and Tudor stables housing a tearoom serving light lunches and home made cakes, are still open.

A former inhabitant, William Knollys, is said to have been Shakespeare's inspiration for Malvolio in *Twelfth Night*. The house was rescued from total neglect by the Brunner family who founded the chemical giant, ICI, in the 1870s. They bought the estate and set about rebuilding work in 1937.

Part of the gardens and medieval tower remains are seen in *Orchis Fatalis*, posing as the monastery in which Brother Robert resides. Barnaby and Scott visit him, asking for help with a crucial translation from Latin, which proves to have rather unusual connotations. For this scene, the gardeners were actually asked to refrain from cutting the grass to give it a wilder look.

ROTHERFIELD PEPPARD - PRIMARY SCHOOL
ALL SAINTS' CHURCH

Peppard in Oxfordshire is part of a trio of villages in the parish of Rotherfield Peppard. Lying close to Henley, another *Midsomer Murders* location, this attractive area comprises of a primary school, church, war memorial hall, two public houses and common flanked by some pretty cottages. The village name is derived from Pipard or Pypard, who once held the manor at Wallingford.

[All Saints' Church]

However, to *Midsomer Murders* aficionados Rotherfield Peppard is most famous for being the location for Badger's Drift Primary School in the early episode *Death's Shadow*. Founded in 1871, this Victorian building sits at the edge of the common, tucked away down a quiet country lane. Surprisingly it was several years until Barnaby and his team were to return to Rotherfield Peppard. Indeed it was not until 2006 that the film crew finally took up residence once more, this time at All Saints' Church for the wedding of Charles and Hilary King in *King's Crystal*. As this proved to be such an excellent location they made another visit the following year to film the marriage of the pompous Sir Edward Fitzroy to Beth Porteous in *Blood Wedding*. All Saints' Church dates back to Norman times, though a great deal of restoration was carried out in 1875, with significant additions in 1908. Thankfully the church still retains some of its original features, including the chancel which exhibits several pieces of Norman architecture.

THAME - CORNMARKET
TOWN HALL
SPREAD EAGLE HOTEL
MARKET SQUARE
OXFAM BOOKSHOP
NORTH STREET

Thame, pronounced 'Tame' with a silent 'h', takes its name from the nearby River Thame (not as J. R. R. Tolkien claimed in his story *Farmer Giles of Ham* from its resident tame dragon!). Founded in Anglo-Saxon times at a river crossing, this market town is located just off the county border between Oxfordshire and Buckinghamshire. It has a population of around twelve thousand and has been twinned with Montesson in France since 2001. Its Royal Charter for a weekly market, which is still being held today, was granted in 1230.

Mentioned in the Domesday book, the town grew to service the nearby Cistercian monastery at Thame Park. Like many others, the monastery itself fell victim to the Dissolution of the Monasteries during Henry VIII's reign. However, the Church of St. Mary the Virgin, dating from about 1240, still remains. During the English Civil War of the 1640s, Thame was occupied in turn by both Royalists and Parliamentarians. Oliver Cromwell's cousin, John Hampden, died at the former Greyhound Inn, after the battle of Chalgrove in 1643.

Visitors should not miss the medieval Birdcage public house in High Street. Dating back to the 1300s, it is listed as one of the most haunted public houses in England – not surprising considering its former uses which included detaining thieves, housing lepers, and later in history, French officer prisoners during the Napoleonic wars.

The 18th century brought wealth to the town, but the 19th century saw an economic downturn and a workhouse had to be established at nearby Rycote College.

In 1940, a local truck driver discovered a hoard of gold coins and rings whilst walking along the riverbank. These were thought to be at least four hundred years old and are now on display at the Ashmolean Museum in Oxford.

Haddenham & Thame Parkway railway station opened in 1987, linking the town to both Marylebone in London and Birmingham in the Midlands. This replaced the old Thame railway station that closed in the 1960s. The long and varied history of Thame is in evidence throughout the town, with architectural styles from virtually every period from the 13th century onwards.

Every year in September, Thame Showground hosts the United Kingdoms largest one-day agricultural event, the Oxfordshire County and Thame Show. Thame Fair opens for three days at the same time in the town centre.

The town is home to Robin Gibb (of the band The Bee Gees) and Jack Bevan (of the band Foals), while the BBC Radio 2 presenter Ken Bruce lives in a neighbouring hamlet.

So far, Thame has welcomed the *Midsomer Murders* crew ten times – the episodes *Shot at Dawn, Midsomer Life, Picture of Innocence, The Maid in Splendour, Things That Go Bump in the Night, Dead in the Water, The House in the Woods, Vixen's Run, Blood Wedding* and *Days of Misrule* all had scenes set in this market town.

The Cornmarket area was seen in *Dead in the Water*, being the location for the jewellers shop, and in the same episode, the *Midsomer Murders* crew set up a street cafe in a small alleyway halfway down the street for Barnaby and Scott to enjoy a coffee. However, a search for the café would be fruitless since it only exists in Midsomer county. In *The House in the Woods*, Harriet Davis Estate Agents was located here, while the area was again featured in a *Picture of Innocence*, when Barnaby sits inside a small café (this one actually exists), with the infamous kissing scene taking place nearby[1]. The shop that posed as Madrigals camera shop can be found near the market area – in real life, however, it sells something a lot more palatable than cameras, namely chocolate! A real

---

[1] Barnaby is accosted by a stranger who pretends she knows him, giving him a big hug and kiss. This is captured on camera, digitally altered to appear as an ex-girlfriend of Barnaby's, and later displayed at the Luxton Deeping's annual photographic exhibition, much to the embarrassment of Tom and Joyce Barnaby who are in attendance.

camera shop at the corner of Cornmarket Street stood in for the Fixpix Photo Shop, allegedly located in Causton.

Readers may be able to spot the courtyard used by the funeral parlour in *Things That Go Bump in the Night* and seen in *Vixen's Run*. Thame Town Hall at the other end of the High Street has posed both as Causton Arts Centre for the art exhibition that Scott and Cully visit together in *The Maid in Splendour*, and the Mayor's office in *Shot at Dawn* – Jones and Barnaby (who rather impossibly managed to get a parking space just opposite the door!) can be seen leaving the building early on in the episode. Joyce can also be seen singing carols outside the Town Hall in *Days of Misrule*.

The Georgian Spread Eagle Hotel in High Street, with its massive signpost in front, also featured, but under a pseudonym. In *Midsomer Life*, it appears under the guise of The Morecroft Hotel where hotel rooms, parking area and the bar were used in some scenes – most memorably the fight between the 'Metro Tossers' and the locals in the bar, where Barnaby gets hit on the nose when he gets involved.

The *Midsomer Life* office is walking distance away in Market Square; it is the former Thame Tourist Office (now the Citizens Advice Bureau) and also houses the public conveniences. The *Midsomer Murders* crew took over the vacant office for three days in 2007 and decorated it with specially produced editions of *Midsomer Life* magazines and also a very 'Midsomerian' stuffed badger.

[The *Midsomer Life* office]

Funnily enough, when Barnaby and Jones arrest the killer and lead the guilty party out to the waiting police car, they are in fact coming out of the public toilets! This building also appeared as Causton Library in *Vixen's Run*. In the same episode, Lucinda and Simon are also seen meeting up outside The Swan Hotel, however, curiously the interior scenes where actually shot at the Spread Eagle Hotel & Restaurant.

Jenny's Cover to Cover bookshop is a real bookshop, a rarity in *Midsomer Murders*, where buildings and shops often change their usage.

The crew took over the Oxfam bookshop in High Street to film the scenes.

A bookbinders in North Street became the printers for Cully's wedding service cards. Barnaby and Jones rush to pick these up at the last minute in *Blood Wedding* with Jones breaking Barnaby's credit card while trying to force an entry to the premises. Finally, Cully tries her wedding dress on in a bridal wear shop in Thame.

THE HASELEYS - THE PLOUGH PUBLIC HOUSE
ST. PETER'S CHURCH
VILLAGE HALL

For centuries, only woods covered the areas where Great and Little Haseley now lie, so the name is thought to derive from Hazel Ley, meaning 'a clearing in a hazel wood'. Many of the houses date back to the 17th century, however, it is believed that some parts of The Haseleys were founded in Saxon times.

Sheep farming was the main source of income during the Tudor era. There were also several thriving shops and businesses at one time, though sadly these have long since disappeared. The charming Oxfordshire villages of Great and Little Haseley have proved perfect locations for Midsomer country. Several of the pretty thatched cottages were used as homes for the residents of Goodmans Land in *Dark Autumn* and the local public house, The Plough, was home to John Field. In the garden, an 'Aunt Sally' game can be found. Played only at public houses in Oxfordshire, Barnaby and Troy partake of this game in *Dark Autumn* – with Barnaby obtaining an almost impossible score!

Several cottages were also used as homes for dubious *Midsomer Murders* residents in *Picture of Innocence, Midsomer Rhapsody, Hidden Depths* and *Days of Misrule*.

Robert de Gaston, an Abbot of Abingdon, who died in the village in 1331, built the chancel at St. Peter's Church in Great Haseley. There are also Norman arches in the south and west doorways. The church was used for the wedding scenes in *Midsomer Rhapsody* and the somewhat more sombre postman's funeral in *Dark Autumn*.

There is a manor house close to the church that was originally built in the 1600s, however, it was largely rebuilt around 1700. Unfortunately, although parts of it can be seen from a footpath, it is not open to the public.

Great Haseley's village hall has also been made great use of during the course of the series. First seen as an antique shop in *Dark Autumn*, it then went on to become the venue for the book-signing session in *The Fisher King*, the photographic exhibition in *Picture of Innocence* and Midsomer Parva village hall in *Blood Wedding*.

A private residence, whose topiary gardens are sometimes open to the public, in Little Haseley became the opulent residence of Melvyn Stockard in *Who Killed Cock Robin?* and later Noah Farrow's house in *Midsomer Rhapsody*.

TURVILLE - ST. MARY THE VIRGIN CHURCH
TURVILLE SCHOOL
BULL AND BUTCHER PUBLIC HOUSE

[Not just *Midsomer Murders* but *The Vicar of Dibley* too!]

Nestling at the bottom of the Hambleden Valley, about five miles from Henley on the Buckinghamshire/Oxfordshire border, this picturesque village seems to be stuck in a time warp. Its name derives from the

Anglo-Saxon words *thyrre* and *feld*, which means 'dry open land'. It is listed in the Anglo-Saxon Chronicle in 796 as Thyrefeld. Roman gold coins found locally in the 18th century point to a previous Roman settlement.

The manor of Turville once belonged to the abbey at St. Albans, but was dissolved under Henry VIII in 1547. The manor house has since been rebuilt as Turville Park, a fine stately home in nearby Turville Heath. The present inhabitant of the manor is Lord Sainsbury, of the J. Sainsbury plc supermarket family.

The church, dedicated to St. Mary the Virgin, is a low-slung flint building with stone dressings and an old tile roof, dating back to the 10th century, and lies opposite the small village green, right in the heart of this community. Comedy fans will instantly recognise the church as the one from the television series, *The Vicar of Dibley*, the church in which Geraldine Granger looked after her flock.

On top of the hill, overlooking Turville, is Cobstone Mill, often mistakenly called Turville Windmill, a smock mill built in 1816 as a replacement for the original 16th century postmill. Just to complete the confusion, it doesn't belong to the village, but is actually part of Ibstone. It was a working mill until 1873, but was subsequently damaged by fire and deteriorated. The film world came to its rescue in 1967, when *Chitty Chitty Bang Bang*, starring Dick Van Dyke as the inventor Caractacus Potts, who creates a flying car, used the mill as the family's home. It was restored for filming, and sold afterwards, and is still in private hands today.

The local public house, The Bull and Butcher, is quintessentially English, offering two main areas inside, both with big open fires and original beams, and a large sunny garden. During the week, it has some remarkable items on its menu – a dish of Dibley Pudding, Chitty Chitty Bangers & Mash and a Midsomer Burger! There is a picture of Barnaby, Scott and the staff behind the bar.

Further productions that used Turville include *Goodnight Mister Tom*, which starred the indomitable John Thaw, *Went the Day Well?* (in which German paratroopers invade a small English village) filmed in 1942, *Father Came Too!* filmed in 1963, *The New Avengers* episode *House of Cards* came here in 1976 with Steed fighting near the windmill, *Little Britain* filmed the Daffyd Thomas scenes here (not in Wales!), *Miss Marple*, *Foyle's War*, *Jonathan Creek* … in fact the list is almost endless.

81

Of course, this lovely village has also been a big draw for the *Midsomer Murders* crew, most notably in *The Straw Woman* where it became Midsomer Parva. The exterior shots of the church were all filmed here, though curiously another church was used for the interior scenes. Turville school posed as the village hall while one of the cottages was used as Liz Francis' house and the 'Straw Woman' of the title was burnt on the green. The pretty village centre and some of the cottages were also used in *Murder on St. Malley's Day*, along with the public house, which became The Chalk and Gown. Also, in *Dark Autumn*, there are some beautiful views of the village as Barnaby talks to Louise August in a field near the windmill.

WALLINGFORD - THE CORN EXCHANGE

[Causton Playhouse]

The nearby River Ford drew the first settlers to the area during the Bronze and Iron Ages. The Romans followed in their footsteps, but it was the Anglo-Saxons that built the first town here. In fact St. Leonard's Church still has some surviving Anglo-Saxon features. Due to the threat posed by Viking invaders in the 9th century, the Saxon King Alfred fortified the town, then as large as Alfred's capital, Winchester. Today's inner town street layout is still based on that of Alfred's time.

In 1066, the Normans chose Wallingford to be the site of a massive castle, which dominated its history for the next six hundred years. Henry II granted the town a Charter of Liberties in 1155, one of the oldest in England. This was a thank you for supporting his mother, Queen Matilda, during her conflict with Stephen over the English throne during the 12th century Civil War. After this period, Wallingford was closely linked to the English Royal families and their history, taking the King's side during the Civil War against Oliver Cromwell. When he won, Cromwell's council ordered the demolition of the castle.

Wallingford eventually became a market town, attracting a railway link at nearby Cholsey in 1866. Unfortunately, it fell victim to Dr. Beeching's streamlining of the railways and was forced to close in 1959. However, the line has since had a reprieve and is presently run by the Cholsey & Wallingford Railway Preservation Society as a tourist attraction.

The town's most famous son is Judge Blackstone, born in 1723. He attended the well-known Charterhouse school in London, and read Civil Law at Pembroke College, Oxford. In 1763, he became Solicitor General to George III's wife, Charlotte. Whilst resident at Wallingford, he wrote the internationally famed law books. After 1776, his Commentaries formed the basis of the new United States Constitution and legal system, his name is therefore familiar to most citizens of the United States of America.

Wallingford to *Midsomer Murders* aficionados is, of course, the original Causton, Barnaby's home and beat.

The Corn Exchange was built in 1856 and this theatre and cinema is home to the Sinodun Players. The world famous detective writer, Dame Agatha Christie, was a former president. The creator of Hercule Poirot and Miss Marple lived on the outskirts of the town for some forty years and is buried in Cholsey churchyard. Situated on the east side of the Market Place, The Corn Exchange is well known to *Midsomer Murders* fans as the Causton Playhouse. It appeared as such in four episodes, namely *Death of a Hollow Man, Strangler's Wood, Death's Shadow* and *Death of a Stranger*. In several instances, members of the Sinodun Players were used as extras. Who could forget the scene in *Death of a Hollow Man*, when, during the performance of Peter Schaffer's *Amadeus*, the lead character commits involuntary suicide on stage?

The local choir can also be seen and heard in several episodes, for example in *Death in Chorus* as the Midsomer Worthy Choir, together with Joyce and Dr. Bullard, and later even Jones, who proves an excellent substitute after Joyce hears him singing in the shower!

Further *Midsomer Murders* locations include a record shop close to The Corn Exchange, the front of the Town Hall and around the market square. This area also puts in an appearance in *The Black Book*.

[The perfect place for a riverside drink]

The gardens of a private house on the banks of the River Thames posed as a public house garden first visited by Cully and Simon Fletcher in *Death's Shadow*. It also reappeared in *Dead Man's 11* with the Barnaby's enjoying a drink in the grounds. In *Blue Herrings*, Troy and Barnaby go into Payne's Jewellers, which used to be located in the 9th century lane off the market square. Wallingford's famous bridge, also seen in *Midsomer Murders*, is only a short stroll away.

WARBOROUGH - VILLAGE GREEN
THAME ROAD
SIX BELLS ON THE GREEN INN
CRICKET PAVILION

Warborough has one of the largest village greens in Oxfordshire. Surrounded by so many pretty houses and thatched cottages, it has proved to be a perfect location for the fictional world of *Midsomer Murders*. The village name derives from the Anglo-Saxon for 'Watch Hill'. It is believed this was due to a place called 'Town Hill', an excellent look-out point, which lies to the north of Warborough. Parts of the church date back to 1666, though sadly, this hasn't been used in the series to date.

The village is first appeared in *Market for Murder*, where Barnaby and Troy are seen driving around the green. One of the village cottages also becomes a newsagent, famously being the shop where Troy secretly buys a copy of *The Hawk*, then wrapping it in a newspaper to keep it hidden from Barnaby's eyes. Later the same cottage actually becomes a dolls shop in *Bad Tidings* and reappears as a Post Office and village store in *The Great and the Good*.

In Scott's first episode, *Bad Tidings*, the real Warborough newsagent and village store in Thame Road, close to the green, becomes his first *Midsomer Murders* home, when he rents a flat above the shop. Charles Rust's home, and Jacob Stoke's stack (sadly now demolished) were also in Warborough, and the Open Garden Day, 'Midsomer Mallow in Bloom', was held on the village green. The Six Bells on the Green Inn sits quietly tucked away at the side of the green making it a wonderfully secluded location for filming.

This 16th century thatched inn appears in *Bad Tidings* and *Left for Dead* under its real name, and in the guise of The Luck in the World in *Second Sight*, The Quill Inn in *Sins of Commission* and finally The Black Swan in *The Great and the Good*.

[The Six Bells on the Green Inn]

Cottages along the green can also seen in *The House in the Woods* and *Left for Dead*, as well as in *Second Sight*, where one house becomes

85

Lucky Lol Tanner's Betting Shop and another was turned into a public house called The Swan in *Left for Dead*.

The cricket pavilion becomes Badger's Drift village hall in *The Great and the Good*. This was once used as a schoolroom for children that were evacuated from London during World War II.

In true *Midsomer Murders* fashion, The Warborough and Shillingford Festival has been held on the village green almost every year since 1965. Events have included a church fete, a village rounders championship, traditional side shows with various bands and musical offerings.

WATLINGTON - HIGH STREET
ST. LEONARD'S CHURCH
TOWN HALL
LIBRARY

With just under three thousand inhabitants, Watlington is the smallest market town in England. Sitting at the foot of the Chiltern Hills, it was first recorded as a Saxon settlement in the 8th century, but is believed to be older. Its name derives from the Celtic for 'settlement of Waecel's people' and in the Doomsday book it is listed as Watelintone. This actually indicates that Watlington existed in some form from the 6th century onwards.

It is close to junction six of the M40, just after the Chiltern escarpment – Rosemary Thurman can be seen travelling through this scenic part of the motorway in *Judgement Day* whilst talking on her mobile, remarking "I'm on the M40". The town is skirted by the Icknield Way, part of The Ridgeway National Trail, which stretches between the Neolithic stone circles of Avebury in Wiltshire and Ivinghoe Beacon in Buckinghamshire.

Watlington has many historical buildings, particularly along High Street which is lined with shops and houses from the 15th, 16th and 17th centuries. There have also been a surprisingly high number of public houses for such a small town – around a dozen buildings have links to this trade.

The town provided several locations for the *Midsomer Murders* crew. The butchers shop in High Street stood in for Ray Dorset's Butchers in

Judgement Day, the episode which, incidentally, starred a then largely unknown Orlando Bloom (who later appeared in such blockbusters as *Pirates of the Caribbean* and *Lord of the Rings*).

St. Leonard's Church dates back to the 12th century, although what the visitor sees today dates mainly from 1877, when it was rebuilt. The white mark on Watlington Hill, above the town, was created in 1764, and designed by local squire Edward Homer, who thought it would give the impression that the church had a spire when seen from his home. The church was used in *Ring Out Your Dead*. However, the ringing chamber seen in this episode is actually that at Bray in Berkshire, while the actual bells heard are from a church in Monks Risborough, Buckinghamshire.

The Granary on High Street, a unique timber building on saddle stones that was once used as a grain store, appeared in *Midsomer Rhapsody* as Harvey Crane's Antiques. The Town Hall, seen in *Judgement Day,* was built in 1665 as a market hall and boys school, to commemorate the reinstatement of the monarchy after the Civil War had ended.

[The Town Hall]

In *A Tale of Two Hamlets*, a lane leading off High Street was turned into run-down Lower Warden, including imported rubbish and a scruffy cat, courtesy of the *Midsomer Murders* crew. The Watlington branch library, near the war memorial, is seen in the background as Causton library in *Orchis Fatalis* when Scott visits Cully, then working at one of her many jobs, in Midsomer Travel (actually the local estate agents). The estate agents was also used as Beauvoisin Estates in the earlier episode *Dead Man's 11*. Watlington can also be spotted by eagle-eyed viewers in *Sins of Commission.*

Are you a Location Detective? ... Then you should discover our range of Location Guides ...

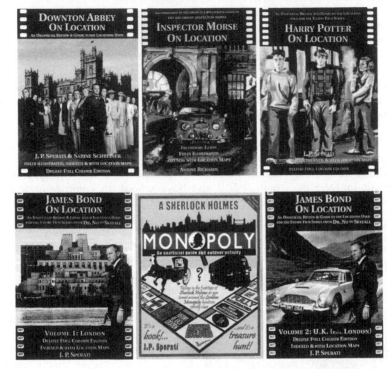

PLACES INDEX

Churches, Abbeys & Other Ecclesiastical Buildings

Hotels, Inns, Public Houses & Restaurants

Museums, Stately Homes & Other Tourist Attractions

Preserved Railways

EPISODE INDEX